HOW TO GET PUBLISH
WIN RESEARCH FUND...

Most journal articles and research proposals are rejected. That represents a waste of everyone's time, energy, and spirit, especially now when, more than ever, academic careers are precarious. In this practical book, Professor Abby Day addresses these two inter-related and most challenging areas for academics and researchers in their professional careers: how to secure research funding and how to get research published.

Reviewers, unpaid and often unappreciated, are over-stretched with their regular academic jobs, and increasingly reluctant to spend time reading poorly constructed papers or proposals. As fewer reviewers are available, the waiting time for a decision increases. Everyone loses. It doesn't have to be like that. Professor Day's ground-breaking strategy covers both publishing and funding challenges in similar, yet distinct ways. Lack of time? Conflicting priorities? No idea where to start or what matters most? This book explains how to overcome these and other common obstacles to successful publication and funding. For the first time, one book covers both activities, with practical guidance for setting your strategy and purpose, identifying the right publisher or funder, and understanding your audience and the key criteria for success, as well as helpful advice for writing and managing the challenges of an academic career. This book draws on the first and second editions of two international bestsellers, *How to Get Research Published in Journals* and *Winning Research Funding*. Based on original research with editors, funders, and successful academics, plus two decades of running international workshops on publishing and funding, Professor Day has now updated and merged these two critically acclaimed texts.

This book is essential reading for graduate students and early career faculty members, who will gain new and effective insights and strategies to secure funding and publication opportunities to help develop their academic careers.

Abby Day is Professor of Race, Faith and Culture in Sociology, Goldsmiths, University of London, UK. Before entering academe, Abby spent 20

HOW TO GET PUBLISHED AND WIN RESEARCH FUNDING

Abby Day

Routledge
Taylor & Francis Group

LONDON AND NEW YORK

Designed cover image: © Getty Images / elenabs

First published 2023
by Routledge
4 Park Square, Milton Park, Abingdon, Oxon OX14 4RN

and by Routledge
605 Third Avenue, New York, NY 10158

Routledge is an imprint of the Taylor & Francis Group, an informa business

British Library Cataloguing-in-Publication Data
A catalogue record for this book is available from the British Library

Library of Congress Cataloging-in-Publication Data
Names: Day, Abby, 1956– author.
Title: How to get published and win research funding / Abby Day.
Description: Abingdon, Oxon ; New York : Routledge, 2023. |
Includes bibliographical references and index. |
Identifiers: LCCN 2022057688 (print) | LCCN 2022057689 (ebook) |
ISBN 9781032195452 (hardback) | ISBN 9781032195445 (paperback) |
ISBN 9781003259718 (ebook)
Subjects: LCSH: Scholarly publishing. | Academic writing. | Proposal writing for grants. | Proposal writing in research. | Research grants.
Classification: LCC Z286.S37 D39 2023 (print) | LCC Z286.S37 (ebook) |
DDC 808.02—dc23/eng/20230302
LC record available at https://lccn.loc.gov/2022057688
LC ebook record available at https://lccn.loc.gov/2022057689

ISBN: 978-1-032-19545-2 (hbk)
ISBN: 978-1-032-19544-5 (pbk)
ISBN: 978-1-003-25971-8 (ebk)

DOI: 10.4324/9781003259718

Typeset in Garamond
by codeMantra

Printed in the United Kingdom
by Henry Ling Limited

CONTENTS

PREFACE

This book is an updated version of *How to Get Research Published in Journals* and *Winning Research Funding*.

When I first wrote *How to Get Research Published in Journals* in 1986 I was a professional editor and publishing consultant. In 1999 I decided to move into academe full time, returning as a 'mature' student to university where I took an MA and then a PhD in Religious Studies at Lancaster University in the UK, focusing on the sociology of religion. I then researched and wrote *Winning Research Funding* in 2002 and updated *How to Get Research Published in Journals* in 2007. At the time of writing I am Professor of Race, Faith and Culture in the Sociology Department at Goldsmiths, University of London.

For the first time, one book covers both activities, drawing on the second and first editions of those two books, based on original research with editors, funders, and successful academics, plus two decades of running international workshops on publishing and funding.

I was struck by the awful realization that most articles and research proposals are rejected. That represents a waste of everyone's time, energy, and spirit, especially now when, more than ever, academic careers are precarious. Reviewers, unpaid and often unappreciated, are over-stretched with their regular academic jobs, and increasingly reluctant to spend time reading poorly constructed papers or proposals. As fewer reviewers are available, the waiting time for a decision increases. Everyone loses.

This book is a merger of several revised chapters from *How to Get Research Published in Journals* (HGRPJ) (2nd edition 2008) and *Winning Research Funding* (WRF) (1st edition 2003). Both titles have sold well and met with good reviews. The new book merges much material from both texts and updates the examples throughout. It retains its primary focus on journals, as the most valuable form of publication for people wanting to enhance their reputation, while offering occasional insights into book publishing as appropriate.

When the original book *HGRPJ* was published (1998), academics were still reading journals in the library and therefore had a tangible, close understanding of what a journal is. Now, libraries don't even stock paper journals and few students or early career academics ever visit the online site, preferring instead to keyword search for a particular paper and download that. This means that the latest generation of academics have a disconnected, disembodied engagement with journals and are ill-prepared for publishing when they know so little about the journal or its community.

Further, there are many technological developments concerning paper and proposal submission, publicity, production, and collaboration, as well as name changes and new important bodies in the field. This has required chapter-by-chapter updating and revision. Open Access and proliferation of publishing sites provide new opportunities and also hidden dangers for those not prepared for the sometime unscrupulous activities.

There are primarily four new developments with which this volume engages:

1. In teaching with the books and running workshops at universities worldwide, I realized increasingly that people interested in publishing are also interested in funding and that my key success factors for each overlap considerably. They are all linked in what I describe as an interdependent virtuous 'Circle of Success' underpinning a successful academic career: publications strengthen chances of obtaining research funding, which produces more publications, all building an author's and institution's reputation, leading to more research funding and publications. This forms the basis of the new Chapter 1 The Circle of Success.

2. Chapters 4 and 5 address the long-ignored 'elephant in the room' about the ethics of publishing and funding. Questions are being asked throughout the academy about how the knowledge we produce can be 'decolonized'. This book acknowledges those issues, highlighting areas where publications and funding experiences are unequal and how some people are trying to address this.

3. Because the academic world is increasingly unstable, many early career researchers will depend on research funding for their jobs. This means they now must manage their careers as a series of short-to-medium term projects. This book addresses that reality and discusses how people manage their careers as contract, fixed-term researchers and take a strategic approach to publications. This idea is woven throughout and covered in a new substantial section in Chapter 3,

Why do you want research funding?, and Chapter 12, Managing relationships and academic careers.

4. Novice authors and researchers often fail to appreciate how much they, not their publisher or funder, will need to do to publicize their work. This is addressed in detail in Chapter 12, where a section on 'being your own publicist' discusses creating strategies that will ensure the work is being read and seen by the people who matter most, mainly focusing on social media, launches, and conferences.

During my career I became associated with the British Sociological Association where I was a Trustee with special responsibilities for publications, working closely with Sage Publishing. I then moved onto being a Trustee with special responsibilities for publications with the Sociological Review Foundation. Both experiences gave me new opportunities to consider publications more widely, in new networks and with new technologies. I was therefore delighted to be given the opportunity to review these two books and expand and update key sections.

I also benefitted from reading the many reviews this book has received in the past ten years. Most were gratifyingly positive and where there was criticism, I have tried to take the comments constructively into this new edition – apart from one which referred to my somewhat relentlessly breezy, cheery tone. For that I make no apologies: I have facilitated too many workshops with nervous and fearful novice writers to make any changes to what I hope is an enthusiastic and encouraging 'voice'.

Much, of course, has remained the same because, largely, the world of academe and publishing still operates in much the same way. This is a community of scholars – teachers and researchers – devoted to learning and discovery and to sharing what they have learned and discovered. One way they do that is through publishing in journals and the other is to participate in different kinds of collaborations through funded research. This book is designed to show you how to do both.

Abby Day
London 2023

PART I
SETTING A STRATEGY

1 INTRODUCTION
A circle of success

Introduction

Becoming a published academic is both a dream and necessity; being funded these days may be a way to increase visibility and value for some, or the only means of doing academic work for others. Since the first edition of *How to Get Research Published in Journals* was published in 1986, its second edition in 2008 and *Winning Research Funding* published in 2003, I have engaged with academics worldwide, in many disciplines, and at different stages in their careers. Some people I first met as my students, others as my mentors, and many more as participants in workshops and webinars. For many years I hosted separate events – one for getting published, and another for getting funded. Increasingly, it became less coherent to separate those two strands. At a writing workshop, people often asked my advice for getting funded, and at funding workshops, people wanted to know how to increase their chances of publication.

As academic life changed from an expectation of steady work and tenure to something now much more precarious, becoming a well-published author and a funded researcher was no longer options for those who had the time and inclination to write yet another paper and submit yet another funding proposal. For many early career scholars, their only hope for employment was a series of short-term, funded projects for which evidence of a good publication record was a necessary part of their proposal and any hope for success.

Many novice academics are unaware of one of the most important aspects of their publishing career: anything they send to a journal must be original. This means that if in their haste to be published following a PhD they have already published their thesis as a book, they have likely ruined their chances of being published in a top journal.

And so, as I introduced key points and answered questions at separate publishing and funding events it became obvious that much of my advice

DOI: 10.4324/9781003259718-2

was the same, whether they were asking about being published or funded. The detail, of course, differed: which journals I might recommend or what funding body seemed most appropriate for them would change depending on their career stage or discipline. But those details were, I knew, necessary but insufficient conditions for success. What they really needed to know, and to practise, were the fundamental principles that governed both activities: how and where in their overall strategy did those options fit? And, yes, we were all impressed that they could list all their methods, show how their research fit into a wider body of literature, itemize their findings, and demonstrate their validity, but so what? Why did it matter, and to whom? How well did they understand their own originality and contribution to their fields? Who did they want to reach? Who really mattered and why? Who cared?

That is why this current book needed to be written. Those stories needed to be told. I knew that only by combining the shared principles of both publishing and funding, and then diving deeper into the detail each required, would the needs of early, mid- and even later career academics be met. Most importantly, only by bringing together the different aspects of publishing and funding could I provide the full picture of what, for every academic, is an inter-locked, inter-dependent Circle of Success.

As an academic gets published, that success feeds into a research proposal and increases the chances of funding; those two activities increase

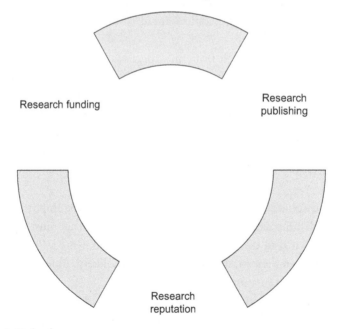

Research funding

Research
publishing

Research
reputation

Figure 1.1 Circle of success.

an academic's visibility and reputation as a researcher; the funded project opens dissemination routes, including publications, which once more enhance their profile and strengths for being funded. And so, the cycle continues.

It is important to note that, despite the sense of precarity and competition that pervades academe today, it was in some ways ever thus. Academics are reading and publishing research in academic journals for much the same reason as they have since 1665, when the first scientific journal in the English-speaking world, *The Philosophical Transactions of the Royal Society*, was launched. Academics seek money for funded projects as academics and artists have for centuries. In the 16th century, the Medici family in Florence were both bankers and popes. Without them, the world would never have seen the glories of Michelangelo. British artist Damien Hirst was first funded by Charles Saatchi who co-owned an advertising agency. A 2019 report by Arts Council England (Private Investment in Culture Survey 2019) showed that more than 90 per cent of arts and culture organizations had received in the previous year some kind of funding from the private sector. In most countries, the private sector funds most scientific research, followed by research councils.

Those examples are not exhaustive, but my point is to show that most research has always been, and still is, funded. Further, it would be spurious, and a great disservice to many fine academics, to suggest that funded research is somehow less worthwhile, or less 'objective' or 'independent' than unfunded research. There has always been poor research, biased research, and falsified findings, but the source of its funding is not, I suggest, the causal variable. It is perfectly possible to produce shoddy work without external funding. And for those who eschew external funding and depend on time and resources from the university department, why would they be unmarked by wider pressures and expectations? The way most research contracts are created and executed makes it unlikely that a funder will intervene to cover up or change results to suit its own objectives. Nevertheless, problems can occur, and these are discussed in future chapters. For now, my point is simply to convey that getting published and funded are the twin, conjoined activities that have always fuelled academe and likely always will. The purpose of this book is to share the success and failure stories that can help academics navigate this sometimes difficult and largely unfamiliar terrain.

I now want to review current practices of journal publishing and external funding to highlight what has changed recently, what is likely to change, what will likely remain the same, and why any of that may or may not matter to any academic.

Academic publishing: trends and changes

There are three main issues driving change – and stability – in the publishing field:

1. Pressures to publish.
2. Places to publish.
3. Profitability of publishing.

Pressures to publish

One major change over the last ten years has been an increased pressure from funders, government, and universities to disseminate more widely. It has become increasingly apparent during the last decade or so that, one way or other, academics must publicize their research. Publicly and privately funded research comes with certain conditions, such as conducting the research ethically, completing it on time and within budget, and – most importantly – disseminating the results. Research councils, charities, and the private sector all stipulate that their funding is linked to dissemination. Some funders may even ring-fence a specific amount of money to pay for dissemination when a project ends. Research councils often tie end-of-award decisions to dissemination. Indeed, specifying how you will do that is one of the most important critical success factors in any funding application.

That is why, as I outlined above, the two activities of funding and publishing are best reviewed together. Even research that is indirectly funded as part of an academic's salary comes with the expectation to publish, which then feeds into an assessment process that determines promotion, or sometimes how much money an institution will receive from government. In the UK, for example, the Research Excellence Framework (REF) is carried out by the UK's higher education funding bodies: Research England, the Scottish Funding Council (SFC), the Higher Education Funding Council for Wales (HEFCW), and the Department for the Economy, Northern Ireland (DfE). Research publications are part of what are known as 'outputs': a publication, a performance, or an exhibition. These are considered according to three criteria: their quality, their impact beyond academia, and the research environment (usually the department or wider institution) that supports the research. The people who make those judgements are academics and members of the wider public who sit on panels of 34 subject areas called 'units of assessment'.

The Higher Education Institutions (HEIs) which score best on the REF receive more funding than those that do not. Indeed, one quarter of central government research income goes to just four UK universities – Oxford, Cambridge, University College London, and Imperial College. That those who have the highest research ratings get more money leads, some argue, to a self-perpetuating structural elitism in education. Public money is not, according to many researchers, distributed fairly amongst institutions. Many people are critical of the REF for this reason, arguing that new universities or those without a long research record and infrastructure to support it can never break through into the 'elite' arena.

This puts more pressure on universities to increase their research profile, and a major strategy to achieve this is through publishing. The pressure to publish is combined with increasing choices of places to publish. In our more global, interactive, digital, instant age, authors are able to choose more and varied routes to dissemination. I will review a few below.

Popular media

Radio, magazines, newspapers, television, and newsletters all offer excellent opportunities for academics to publicize their research. Many funding bodies and universities require researchers to issue press releases and co-operate with in-house public relations experts.

Reports

Most funders expect the Principal Investigator to write a publicly available, final report summarizing the project's key findings. These are usually published in the funder's own newsletters or websites. It may also be appropriate to produce reports for government or other bodies if there are policy issues to be considered.

Social media

People communicate their research via numerous means, from Twitter and Meta to personal and institutional blogs. Here, discussion is largely unmediated, unedited, and seen to be free from more overt forms of commercial or political controls.

Conferences and seminars

Academic conferences and seminars are ideal venues to disseminate research and to network with other researchers, sometimes forging lasting collaborative relationships. Some conferences will publish presentations on their websites and in their newsletters, or issue post-conference journals or edited collections based on the papers. Many researchers use conferences as the first site for presenting their research and then amending their papers for potential journal publication. Seminars, usually smaller and more focused events, provide ideal opportunities to discuss people's research in detail.

Predatory journals

Academics are increasingly receiving unsolicited invitations to publish in journals or edit special issues of journals. If you are an Early Career researcher, receiving such an invitation should be your first clue that something is not quite right. A reputable journal would never approach an unknown academic with a direct invitation to publish or edit a special issue. Any such invitations are made directly from the Editor to a named academic of considerable reputation. So-called 'predatory journals' are concocted by non-academics in order to lure – prey on – unsuspecting authors to send in their manuscripts, for which they will be charged a fee. The result may be something looking like an online publication, with one important difference: no one respects it, or you for being there.

To flesh out more detail about what constitutes a predatory journal, scholars and publishers met in 2019 to discuss this worrying trend and decide what could be done about it. As reported in *Nature*, Grudniewicz et al. (2019), the group agreed with the following definition:

> Predatory journals and publishers are entities that prioritize self-interest at the expense of scholarship and are characterized by false or misleading information, deviation from best editorial and publication practices, a lack of transparency, and/or the use of aggressive and indiscriminate solicitation practices.

They also found that there were few ways to immediately spot the predator, as many have infiltrated reputable databases and have cloaked themselves with an aura of respectability. To help potential authors recognize a predatory journal, the group agreed that there were several revealing characteristics including false information on their websites about, for example, composition of editorial boards and incorrect claims of membership of organizations or indexing systems; lack of transparency; inconsistency and often incorrect spelling or use of grammar; aggressive, indiscriminate, repeated, excessively flattering solicitations. One of their other 'warning signs' is, to me, the most obvious: there is a clear mismatch between the purported scope of the journal and the expertise of the author. This problem easily occurs when the journal and author are not in the same academic community. That is why, as I discuss in detail throughout this book, it is important to develop a coherent and sustainable strategy about who the main audiences are for your work, and where you are most likely to find them.

Books

Many academics want to publish a book, either as a result of their PhD or other major research project. This can be an excellent way to publicize a large project and can give a satisfying feeling of 'closure' to a lengthy piece of research. Before rushing to write your book, remember that all publishers require detailed proposals: you can visit their websites and look at their templates and helpful suggestions. If they accept your proposal, they will then send it for review to judge from external assessment whether or not there is a market for your proposed book.

Apart from a book you've written, you might also consider contributing a chapter to someone else's book. This usually happens because someone approaches you and invites you to do so. In that event, you must bear in mind that the editor will expect your chapter to fit into the collection as a whole and you may therefore have to adapt your work considerably.

Book publishing does have several disadvantages. It is time-consuming, with little financial compensation unless you've written a best-selling textbook. It will also not reach a large audience, given that academic books sell in the hundreds and low thousands at best, and its content may be digitized and made freely available through the internet. Academic books are often not reprinted once they sell out, and therefore your book may disappear forever.

More worryingly for many academics, books are not subject to the same rigorous review process as are journal papers. And, once the book is published it may become more difficult to publish the content in journals because it is no longer original. Journal websites are clear about the need for originality and exclusivity. Originality: *The Brazilian Journal of Physics* (Submission Guidelines n.d.), for example, states clearly that 'submission of a manuscript implies: that the work described has not been published before; that it is not under consideration for publication anywhere else'.

The Legon Journal of the Humanities (Promoting Access to African Research 1974) makes a similar point, and also calls attention to the practice of self-plagiarism: when authors duplicate their own material they have published elsewhere:

> For all its issues, *LJH* only publishes original contributions (i.e., papers that have not been published elsewhere) and therefore, disapproves of

duplicate publication and multiple submissions of the same paper to different publication outlets. In consonance with best academic practices, it equally takes a very dim view of the illegitimate direct replication of material in the form of plagiarism, including self-plagiarism. The Editorial Board will not only ban authors of plagiarized material from any subsequent association with the journal, but also bring any breach of intellectual property rights to the attention of the contributor's institution.

In summary, while there are many routes to dissemination, academics need to ensure that any they choose to not replicate each other. How academics choose which medium to use will depend on the audience with whom you want to communicate.

Most large-scale research projects will target a mix of media from newsletters, books, and journals to radio, the web, and television. Whatever the mix you choose, it is likely that the most important publication for your academic career will be the academic journal. Unique amongst all media, a journal paper is systematically double- or triple-blind peer-reviewed and, for the most highly rated journals, difficult to get published in, with acceptance rates in the region of 2 to 10 per cent. The draw of scarcity and perceived value therefore serves as the mark of quality and excellence in your field. That is why many academics place journal publishing at the top of their list.

And yet, the nature of what a journal actually is has changed substantially over the past 20 years or so. This change has been driven by both pressures described above – the pressure to publish and the places available – and a third pressure: the profitability of publishing.

Profitability of publishing

In the mid-1990s, people were accessing research mainly through reading paper-based journals and occasionally by finding journal papers on the internet. Today, the reverse is more likely: we read paper-based journals less and download the electronic version more.

It may be helpful here to summarize briefly the process from submission to publication. An author usually submits a paper to a journal via an electronic platform, enters their personal information, submits an abstract, provides a title and keywords, and attaches the paper. The editor (or assistant) is notified by email that a paper has been submitted and the author receives an automatic email acknowledgement. If the editor concludes that the paper meets the editorial objectives of the journal (and much more about this later), then the editor, often with an assistant, selects referees and sends the paper for review. Referees receive an email notifying them a paper is available for review. Referees download the paper, review it, and send their comments through the system to the editor, who makes one of only three possible decisions: accept, revise, or reject. The editor notifies the author.

If the paper is accepted outright – which rarely happens – then the author celebrates, signs forms regarding copyright and warranties, and awaits publication in several months or a year's time. In the case of 'revise', the author should also celebrate (but often sulks – and more about this later) revises, resubmits the paper and, (subject, sometimes, to further review and revision), eventually receives the final paper, known as a 'proof' in the form of a PDF file to check. The journal is then assembled according to its pagination budget and mix of papers, book reviews, research notes, and so on, and signed off by the editor. Many publishers then send their journals to a printer that produces a paper-based version and mails the final copies to subscribers. Numbers are small because most subscribers to academic journals are university libraries, not individuals. Most publishers today are seeking to reduce their print copies as libraries are clearing their shelves and relying on digital versions.

There are also, apart from paper-based traditional academic journals, peer-reviewed digital journals which have only ever existed in digital format and offer added benefits to authors not found in the traditional model. For example, digital journals can be timelier, shortening the interval between submission and publication. Because they are not constrained by space and cost factors, many allow longer papers than would be possible in paper journals – although some editors of electronic journals still maintain word limits in the interest of coherence. Publishing in a digital journal allows more interesting ways to present data in a flexible, electronic format, which may make it more attractive to authors using tables and graphs and wanting to link to other internet-based sources.

Whether existing first as a digital journal or a paper-based, traditional journal, journal content available on the internet is digitally encrypted so that the content is accessible only to subscribers. This is when the perception of 'the journal' may begin to be obscured. Most people accessing a paper on the internet find it through keyword searches, not through navigating through the journal's home page and browsing through the most recent issue. The practice of key-word access may hide the paper's source and, consequently, the means by which it was produced. What is not obvious to the researcher using search engines is that the source of the paper is most often a traditional journal, created initially through the traditional means of submission, peer review, revision, proofreading, and printing described above. While the content may then be read as a single paper on a web page, its original place was likely in a journal alongside six or seven other papers, book reviews, research notes, and an editorial. Recognizing that source is important because it provides the context within which any academic paper is initially judged by the editorial team. Much more about that later.

The drive towards electronic access has caused the issue of ownership to become hotly contested amongst publishers, government, and academics. Journal publishing is expensive but managed well can be highly profitable. The academic publishing industry is tough and precise. Strong publishers survive; others fail. Even non-commercial publishers, such as learned societies, want their journals to make money, often as a means of subsidising other activities of the society. Over the last decade, many small publishers have been acquired by larger ones and the larger ones have acquired each other as the industry consolidates. How journal subscriptions are sold and bought also reflects this consolidation. Subscriptions to scholarly journals are sold largely to librarians, either directly or via an agent. The librarian may take advice from others, such as departments' library committees or from other library users but will make a final choice based on the budget available. The journal may be bought as a single item, but more frequently today it will form part of a package of a number of journals, sometimes shared amongst several institutions in what is known as 'consortia'. Academic papers are then typically made available through different portals, platforms, or gateways shared by universities and the large database aggregators which manage the content. An academic's institutional password is the key to unlock many of these invisible, but sometimes impenetrable, doors.

Now, we enter a battleground where publishers, research funders, government agencies, and a few high-profile academics fiercely contest who has the right to control journal content. One argument is for 'open access', on the basis that research has already been paid for by the research funder or university (and ultimately the taxpayer) and therefore should be freely available to all. The contrary argument is voiced by publishers who claim that they manage the peer review process, invest in sales and marketing, and take financial risks with new journals and therefore should protect their 'investment'. The current compromise between free and closed access is the traffic light model, where commercial publishers can restrict access to subscribers over journal content for a limited time, usually between six and 24 months, after which time academics can post their papers on their own websites or deposit them in Institutional Repositories. Another method is that publication fees become part of a research project's budget, and therefore the funder (often a government research council) pays the fees on behalf of the researcher.

One consequence is that authors who are neither funded nor can afford author submission fees are increasingly denied access to places to publish. See, for example, Paige Mann (2022) for more discussion, and Chapter 5 in this volume. Another consequence is that the pressure to receive research funding increases as academics realize that this is, increasingly, the only way their research papers can be published.

The battle for the rights and profits of publishing will continue to rage. For academics wanting to publish their work, the questions will always be the same: what is the best route to those I need to reach, how will it benefit them and me, and how do I do it in the least amount of time with the most chance of success?

Choices for funding

Let us now consider the landscape of research funding. The researcher is one of the most important people in society. Researchers influence decisions and in so doing, influence lives. As well as providing useful knowledge and sometimes informing government policy and corporate decisions, they influence how we measure and value the outcomes of research itself. But what governs success? Who gets funded and who does not?

When I asked people how research funding is won, I received generally two types of responses. The first is what I would call the 'top tip' list. I asked everyone I interviewed to name, in brief, a few important factors; those which really 'make the difference' between a winning proposal and a lower-quality one. They clustered under ten broad headings that I call the 'ten top tips' and each will be explored through the book:

1. Articulates problem accurately
2. Provides appropriate background
3. Manageable within the time
4. Cost-effective
5. Linked to defined outcomes
6. Seen to make a contribution to the field
7. Clear methodology
8. Concise writing
9. Demonstrates right team approach
10. Has credible academic supervision

This book has been written to make researchers' tasks easier and more fruitful, to understand 'luck' for what it really is – careful positioning and astute judgement. That, more than anything, is what takes the researcher to the right place and the right people at the right time. The book's central proposition is that there is poor, good, and best practice in research funding today. In exploring best practice, we need to go further than our ten top tips. Those are, indeed, the structural components of research best practice, but not its foundation.

Winning research funding consistently depends on concepts like value and partnership. These concepts turn a one-off experience into a long-term, mutually satisfying relationship where both partners benefit equally. The benefits extend far beyond money to prestige, knowledge, and influence. While the top ten tips may seem components of obvious good practice, these success factors are often ignored by people who fail to win funding. This may reflect their inexperience or time pressures. We will be discussing these factors in detail and offering the benefit of many people's experiences. Yet beyond those process-related issues is another question: why, all other things being equal, are some researchers more successful than others? It does not seem enough to simply do well: it is necessary to do better than that. What is the meaning of that 'better'? In other words, what, in research, is best practice?

Research best practice

Some people say it is factors outside the applicant's control that make the difference. Examples of such comments are:

- Themes are designated each year by research councils – how can you know in advance what they will be?
- A proposal just may not have the right 'fit' with the funder.
- Referees may not like you! You may have offended them previously. It's a small world and even so-called blind refereeing processes may be transparent. As one referee remarked: "It's easy to tell who the authors are – they're the ones most frequently referenced".

Several people, as mentioned earlier, told me that their success was a matter of 'luck'. But what is luck? Should we abandon the quest for best practice in favour of astrology? The following is a typical response to my question – 'but what is luck?'. In this case, she was discussing research into a hotly contested topic that had received a lot of public attention:

Well, I mean, there's always a bit of luck. You can never, you know, you haven't got a sort of magic ball to see in the future. You can actually anticipate that this has got the conditions which is likely to lead to controversy, but it doesn't mean that controversy is likely to occur. I mean, of course you can't, but you can have good hunches and our hunches in fact were correct at the time.

I will be illustrating how successful applicants for research funding convert those 'hunches' into what they really are: reasonable judgements built up over time in a field of expertise. Creating winning proposals is about how to develop those 'hunches' into winning research relationships. Of course, there is always a measure of good fortune in any endeavour. Sometimes it is a matter of being in the right place at the right time or hitting the right tone with the right person on the right day. But most of the time it is more than luck.

People who win research funding and the people who fund them agree that for most applicants most of the time luck is not the most important factor: people who win research funding consistently take a different and measurably better approach than those who do not. That 'approach' is something more complex than simply filling out an application form properly, wearing decent clothes for an interview, carefully reading a call for tender, designing a research approach, or writing clearly. Clearly, the 'top tips' are necessary, but often insufficient, conditions of success.

That leads me to the second sort of response I received. Most successful researchers talk more about relationships, proactivity, and partnerships than they do about applications and proposals. This means that researchers need to choose a prospective funder who matches their needs and interests. To work effectively, the relationship needs to be symmetrical and symbiotic.

Imbalanced relationships are flawed from the outset. Recognizing this, many funders choose not to work with researchers whose focus and approach are not compatible with theirs. That is a reasonable and fair decision. Researchers who seek funding from such inappropriate organizations are likely to be disappointed, even if they receive the money they were looking for.

Based on the assumption that research funding can represent mutual long-term benefit to both partners, this book takes a strategic approach. Whether your desired funding is for a small grant or a five-year programme, it is likely you will be spending a significant amount of time on your research and, consequently, on obtaining the funding. In many cases, you will also be involved with your funder during the research and following. This book aims to help you create a context, a process, and an approach which will make those partnerships worthwhile and enjoyable.

One of the strongest temptations challenging those who want funding is to jump into the application stage without thinking through what they are doing and why. I examine in more detail the question of why research funding is important. Not everyone needs it and not everyone wants it. We therefore need to look at research issues, not only from your perspective but also from that of the funders and other stakeholders.

The research may, for example:

- add conceptually to the current body of knowledge through new thinking
- add empirically to the current body of knowledge through new evidence
- expose and correct an error which has been compounded over the years by researchers who failed to see it
- demonstrate a new way of applying the body of knowledge
- help an organization work differently and better.

Even when the themes and priorities have been articulated by the funding body, it is the researcher's task to identify the implications and the result. Funding bodies, public or private, want to see value for money. The researcher who receives funding needs to demonstrate that it will be used appropriately and that the investment will be worthwhile.

Sometimes, applications fail because the budget is beyond anything the funder can meet, but they also fail because the cost estimates are unrealistically low. Those who fund research do not evaluate proposals based on a notion that 'cheapest is best'. They are, by and large, experienced and committed people with good judgement about likely returns on investment, likelihood of successful completion, and the right balance of costs and benefits. Poor budgeting – either too high or too low – may suggest that the applicant has not reviewed the project carefully or is too inexperienced to complete it successfully.

I also take a closer look at how funding bodies work and what motivates them, to help you assess which may be a well-suited partner. Too many researchers rush around looking for a funding partner in a panic-stricken attempt to find money. Many do not find one or, worse (in the long run), find one who is not suitable. What do you really want, and who will want you?

This is the time to think about what you can gain from a research partnership and what you can give. Funders talk more about 'value' than they do about money. The need to deliver value applies to all potential funders, not just the corporate sector. We look in more detail at particular kinds of funders: government, research councils, the European Community, charitable foundations, and professional bodies. Getting to know these people and how they work is a necessary step in forging long-term relationships.

A theme running throughout this book is about creating the relationship. How will you know if this is the right partner, and you can meet their expectations? Assessing a potential partner's needs does not need to be a difficult task. Unfortunately, it is one most often ignored and said to be the most common cause of application rejection: 'we often wonder if academics can read', one funder said bluntly. One successful researcher explained:

> Obtaining funding is an exercise in 'selling' a project or set of ideas to an audience that has a particular set of interests. Within the context of such a process, there is an inevitable degree of compromise, as projects – or at least their initial outline – are adjusted in accordance with the stated priorities of funding bodies.

Maintaining the position of 'relationship' means this is a valuable, enquiring process. This continues into how the relationship develops. Sometimes, research partnerships break down because each party has different expectations. This will apply to the process of carrying out the research as well as its outcomes. How do academics respond when the research question in a call for tender is clearly wrong, or the proposed methodology inappropriate? We explore later how to meet the funder's expectations without compromising your own values or preferred approach.

The task of preparing a proposal and, sometimes, making a presentation, is time-consuming and arduous, but writing and presenting a proposal is unlikely to be rewarded if researchers skip the preparation stages described throughout this book. The proposal and a presentation are stages in the process of successfully winning research funding, not the whole of the process. Some processes include a phase of feedback, where the funder proposes changes or demands reductions in time and money. In some cases, responding to a request for a change leads to more money, not less: it is not always bad news. Feedback from a proposal is free, often excellent, advice. Successful relationships are nurtured. Knowing how to manage the research partnership will often involve new skills and new ways of working.

One of the necessary outcomes of most research projects is publication. This is something which the funder may or may not require; some, for commercial reasons, may even prohibit it, others may demand it. How do researchers satisfy the need to publish within this complex context? This becomes increasingly difficult in an environment where contract research is more prevalent. Here, every moment counts, every day is billed. Researchers who successfully manage both research and writing plan for publication from the outset. It is easier to think through prospective publication routes when the research is fresh and thriving than when it is finished and growing stale. As I described at the outset, publishing and funding decisions are usually intertwined and co-dependent and therefore a thoughtful, strategic approach is most beneficial.

Using this book

This book is designed to help you answer questions and concerns about publishing and funding in a systematic, logical format. It is for people who want and need to be published in academic journals and to win research funding: researchers, students, and members of faculty.

Publishing and funding may seem like a difficult and mysterious business, but they are not. Once you understand how to go about it, and what will determine your success, it becomes a deeply satisfying experience for the author, researcher, and ultimately the reader.

This book is based on original research into what quality standards editors, funding bodies, and reviewers are seeking and the combined experience of many authors, editors, and reviewers. The conclusions they share are widely tested in practice in many different academic disciplines in many different countries. You can therefore be assured that you will be able to apply their advice with confidence.

The book is in three main parts, reflecting the stages authors and funded researchers go through as they work towards successful publication. Part I will help you define your objectives, allowing you to focus on the task ahead with clarity and economy. Part II invites you to understand more deeply the needs of editors, reviewers, funders, and readers so that you can align your objectives with theirs. Part III allows you to pull together all you have learned into a publishable paper or proposal, looking at the detail of getting the paper or proposal right, and managing the publishing and funding process from your paper or proposal to, eventually, your relationship with the larger publishing or funder community. Each chapter ends with action points to help you apply the principles discussed and practise the techniques described.

I urge you to adopt the step-by-step process in its chronological order. The reason many aspiring authors or funded researchers fail is that they throw themselves immediately into the activity of writing without realizing that it is the forethought, analysis, and preparation that determine the quality of the finished product. If you follow the advice, you will find the process of writing an academic paper or proposal interesting and pleasurable. If you adopt the approach recommended here, you can easily write publishable papers and excellent proposals in much less time than you ever thought possible. Most importantly, it will be a rewarding activity benefiting you, your institution, and all those who stand to gain from reading your work.

References

Grudniewicz et al. (2019). 'Predatory journals: no definition, no defence', Nature 576(7786): 210–212. Available at: www.nature.com/articles/d41586-019-03759-y

Private Investment in Culture Survey (2019). Available at: www.artscouncil.org.uk/sites/default/files/download-file/Private%20Investment%20in%20Culture%20Survey%202019.pdf

Promoting Access to African Research (1974). *Legon Journal of the Humanities*. Available at: www.ajol.info/index.php/ljh

Submission Guidelines (n.d.) *Brazilian Journal of Physics*. Available at: www.springer.com/journal/13538/submission-guidelines

UK Research and Innovation. (2005). 'RCUK position on issue of improved access to research outputs'. Available at: www.rcuk.ac.uk/research/outputs/access/

2 WHY PUBLISH (OR NOT?)

Introduction

Ideas are cheap. No one succeeds because they have good ideas. No single person ever became famous, rich or even promoted on the strength of an idea. It was because they did something with their idea that they reached their desired goal.

Have you ever heard people say that they're afraid to write about their research or give a conference paper because someone might steal their ideas? You might have even said it yourself. But remember, an idea is just an idea. The theft of an idea is only a problem if the thief is going to do something with it. Maybe you have heard people say, on seeing some new invention, book title, TV show, or such like, 'I thought of that years ago! If only I'd got round to doing something with it!' The trouble is, they didn't. Someone else did, and that's what makes the difference.

There is a Japanese story of a Zen master who listened patiently to his student describe his current state of near Enlightenment: 'I've discovered, master, that all ideas are just false and artificial constructs!' The master nodded and replied: 'You can carry around that useless idea of yours if you want to.'

The only thing that counts is action. No one really cares about what you think. How would they know? They will only begin to care if you articulate it. If they want to 'steal' your thoughts, let them. Most of them will stay where you were before you decided to put your idea on paper. Most people's ideas stay as just that – ideas.

The world is filled with wannabees, wouldbees, shouldbees, and gosh-I-nearly-did-its. The worlds of academia and business are no different in that regard. Drawers upon drawers are filled with the beginnings of papers and books, half-hearted attempts to put words to paper, only to be interrupted by something *really* important, like the telephone ringing.

Let's not have any delusions about this. Getting published begins with the desire to do so, swiftly followed by action. Like anything else, it depends

DOI: 10.4324/9781003259718-3

on your priorities. If your priority is to write, you will write. If it is not, you probably will not. This book explores ways in which you can direct your energies and organize your priorities to best effect in getting your work published, but it cannot manage your priorities for you. There are many reasons to publish and just as many not to.

Why publish?

Clarity

There are always competing priorities but, at some point, writing has to become number one. Prof. Linda Woodhead shared her experience with me, and as a successful academic: she was, for example, Programme Director of the UK's largest research programme in the sociology of religion, 'Religion and Society'. The five-year programme jointly sponsored by the Arts and Humanities Research Council and the Economic and Social Research Council ran between 2007 and 2012, funding 75 separate projects with a total budget of £12 million. Not many academics were as busy, or as well-published as Prof. Woodhead. One of the reasons she publishes, she says, is that the effort of writing and revising helps her clarify her thoughts:

> Submitting an article to a refereed journal is a wonderful way of getting several distinguished scholars to engage with your work and give you detailed feedback – all for free! Often you will be asked to resubmit with revisions, and though it may be a painful process, the end result is often a better paper.

Writing and revising are an education in themselves. We have to think through our ideas more carefully and structure them more logically as we write. Seeing our ideas or research findings in black and white allows us to confront the obvious and, at times, the obscure. Suddenly, a throwaway line leaps out at us and we think 'Yes! That's the whole point right there! I should put that point at the beginning, not lose it here in the middle.' Or, sometimes, we reread a paragraph or a phrase which makes us feel a little uneasy. It looks so emphatic on the page, but are we really sure we can be so positive about it? Maybe we ought to check our facts again – or at least express the thought in slightly different terms.

Choosing the right words and the right order all takes time, but most of that time is spent in preparation before we sit down to write. Planning may take weeks but, as we explain later in the book, the writing itself need never take more than a few days. A story about American president Abraham

Lincoln illustrates this point. He agreed to give a speech and was asked how much time he needed to prepare. He suggested that he would need a few days for a 20-minute speech, a week for a ten-minute speech, but if they wanted the speech to last two hours then he was ready immediately.

Revisiting

There's nothing like seeing your idea in black and white to make you take it seriously. Did I really say that? Am I sure about this?

Usually, to get it right, you have to get it wrong first. To achieve a finished draft, you have to go through a first and second draft. There is a great temptation to put off writing until you think you have the perfect paper to write. Take advice from those whose research may, indeed, be close to perfect but who will not let their quest for perfection delay their publications. Prof. Christian Grönroos was Professor of Service and Relationship Marketing at the Swedish School of Economics in Helsinki, Finland when I interviewed him for this book. A prolific author and researcher, he has received several international awards and distinctions for his work. He encourages people to publish their work even when there may be potential for further amendments and corrections. He remembers the advice given to him by his own doctoral supervisor: 'There are only two types of articles; those that are perfect and never get published, and those that are good enough and do.'

During the process of writing a paper, whether empirically based or theoretical, you will have the opportunity to re-examine your method, implications, discussion, findings, and all the other components of an academic paper. You may often choose to alter sections then, or you may most likely decide it is good enough for now, send it away for publication, and continue to refine your approach for the next paper. In either case, you have had the opportunity to review your work and either make improvements or note those points which you need to work on next time.

Feedback

Someone is likely to comment on your work either when you show your draft to colleagues or after the paper is published. Of course, that's a very good reason why some people are reluctant to publish, but we'll examine that later. Let's look at the benefits first.

If your field of interest is growing – and let's hope it is – it grows by people adding their evidence and theories as they examine it. Your contribution causes other people to look at the field in a different way and, when they tell you about it, they are adding their ideas or evidence to yours. Another person's perspective can enrich yours. And, if another perspective causes you to reconsider, or even discard, your theory or idea, that's no problem. It is merely another road you have seen and chosen not to take, and you can be thankful that someone pointed it out before you lost your way.

Feedback can lead to collaboration from unexpected sources. Once published, you begin to meet people who know you through your writing. 'I saw your paper in such-and-such journal' a total stranger may say at a conference and will probably offer a constructive comment or another source of information you hadn't considered.

Feedback from others gives the lie to the old expression that you cannot get something for nothing. Consider the refereeing process. Referees are anonymous authorities, appointed by editors, who will recommend that your piece of work will be accepted as is, rejected, or should be revised and resubmitted. Most experienced authors welcome the 'revise' instruction, almost as much as a straight acceptance. 'Revise' feedback usually includes precise comments about which parts of the paper should be revised, and often how. We will explore the whole nature of refereeing later but, for now, it is enough to point out that the referee is most likely to be a respected leader in your particular field, who is freely giving an opinion on how you can improve your work. And it costs nothing.

Self-worth

There are many theories about human motivation. Behavioural psychologist Abraham Maslow said it was all about needs satisfaction which he neatly described as a hierarchy:

1. Survival – food, warmth
2. Safety – security, protection
3. Belongingness – social acceptance
4. Esteem – social recognition
5. Self-actualization – creativity, spirituality

According to this theory, you cannot paint while you are worrying about where your next meal is coming from. A little simplistic when you think about it, but it can suit as a reason to publish and not publish, and it is a reason many people give to explain their inability to make a start. 'I've a lot of things on my mind right now, but in a month or two I'll be less pressured', they might say. We have all said that, only to find that the months roll on and we are as pressured as ever, taking care of the basics and thinking we cannot devote time to the pressure to publish.

By actually publishing your work you will see tangible evidence that you are clever. Nothing breeds success like success and seeing your name in print gives a satisfying frisson of excitement. And don't tell me you don't send a copy to your mum!

When, later on, we explore how to target journals, a number of techniques will be discussed. For now, it's wise to remember that, not surprisingly, the most sought-after journals have the highest rejection rates. It therefore makes good sense not to aim too high at first. There are more journals than you may know about: these will be easier to get into, with editors and reviewers who have more time to discuss your work with you. With the constantly growing numbers of journals there are likely to be several respectable, accessible journals in any given field that the aspiring author can try. Although famous authors will often say that they lived for years with rejections, not many of us want to do that forever. Be kind to your frail ego and do not start by aiming at the stars: it is crowded up there.

Net worth

Publishing itself rarely makes anyone rich, unless you're a best-selling author, but there are tangible benefits that arise as a result.

Research funding, as discussed in Chapter 1, has become increasingly tied to published results. Although you might worry that you will not be accepted by the journals with the highest impact factors, working through the other journals will help you refine your approach, improve your style, and make it more likely that, sooner rather than later, you will become published where you want. Having your papers published makes you more sought after for other reasons too, depending on your field: conferences, workshops, teaching, speeches, and consultancy are all ways to create opportunities for further research. Some publishers and other organizations give awards for best papers, either as cash prizes, scholarships, research funding, or books.

Promotion

It is fair to say that those who publish in the best journals are good at what they do, but are they really so smart and more deserving of that new job or that promotion than you? Yes, in several ways they are, but not just because they are intellectually advanced, but because they are smart with their time management. They have recognized the importance of publishing and got on with it, which is another reason they deserve promotion.

And do they know something you don't know? Yes, to that as well. They know how to write good papers and how to target the right journals.

They know how to prioritize. They know how to transfer ideas from their heads on to paper where others can read them. By the time you finish this book you will know too, because they'll be telling you in the pages that follow. They are not worried you will steal their ideas. They have made it. So can you.

Institutional

Your college or university needs you. More than ever before, institutions are being held accountable for their 'outputs'. One of the measures being applied is the number of papers published in quality journals. Increasingly, institutions are including publishing obligations in contracts. They want to make sure that the people they hire will not just promise to publish, as everyone does, but will actually do it.

Body of knowledge

Whatever your field, from education research to embryonics, you belong to a body of knowledge. The field only grows because people add to it: people like you, who have something to say. If they did not, the field would atrophy, become stale, and perhaps die altogether. That does not mean everything you say must be brilliant or paradigm-busting. Perhaps your contribution is to revisit the body of knowledge with a new perspective or perhaps it is only to synthesize what has remained unsynthesized. At the very least, perhaps all you will do is clarify the current position or cause a minor stir that can provoke debate.

Either way, it is a matter of making the choice of whether to be in or out of it – whether to fish or cut bait, as my American colleagues say. Are you a passenger, or do you add your own energy to driving the machine? You are paid to teach in that body of knowledge, paid to research about it, and paid to contribute to it. Writing up your findings or articulating your concepts is an obligation.

Concurrent publishing

Finally, most well-published authors think of their research as organic: it changes over time and can be improved endlessly. Each time you submit a paper to a journal you think about your work differently. That is why many authors publish papers as their research develops. Sometimes, a paper on the research design itself will be valuable; another might tackle some aspects of the literature; another might discuss emerging findings, and so on. One exception to this practice might be research that is contracted by a commercial organization hoping to produce a patent or product. People in those fields are often reluctant to share their early findings for fear that their colleagues working elsewhere on the same problem or opportunity will see what they're doing and use it to accelerate their own research.

Those who are so affected, and few are, will have to decide what is best for themselves. My advice is to check with your supervisors, sponsors, and research coordinators who will usually be the best judge of whether the potential threats of publications outweigh the opportunities. Prof. Woodhead says of her students in Religious Studies:

> Publishing and writing are like racing cars – you have to practice to be any good at it. That is one reason I encourage research students to try to publish as soon as they can – alongside writing their thesis if at all possible. Having some published articles on your CV will set you apart from people who only have a thesis. If someone has already published, you can be fairly confident they will keep on publishing.

Think of chapters in books which arose from presentations to conferences, or journal papers which were derived from a doctoral thesis. Remember where this chapter began: no one will steal your ideas if you publish work in progress or different forms of your work in different places. Just make sure you're not using the fear of being copied as an excuse not to publish. After all, there are many more excuses available, as we shall see in the next section.

Why not publish?

I am often impressed with the effort many publishers make to encourage publication even amongst the least inexperienced. Many journals offer prizes specifically targeted to students. The Editorial Advisory Committee of the *Australian Journal of Botany*, for example, offers an annual student prize for the best student-authored paper published in the journal. The rules state:

> To be eligible, the student must be the lead author of the paper, and the paper must be submitted for publication while the student is enrolled for a higher degree, or within two years of graduating for a higher degree.

The material benefits are generous – a one-year personal print/online subscription to the journal, and a AUS$250 book voucher from Csiro Publishing. But my hunch is that the recognition which comes from the prize is unquantifiable. Simone Farrer, Managing Editor, agrees. She told me that 'apart from the monetary value, it is considered a very valuable thing to have on one's CV'. She explained that she introduced the *Australian Journal of Botany* student prize in 2002, to encourage young researchers to publish their work in the journal, and subsequently introduced the student prize for the other journal for which she has responsibility, *Australian Systematic Botany*.

If previously unpublished students have the self-confidence to submit papers to an academic journal, what is stopping everyone else? The central issue is 'going public': the word 'publish' derives from the Latin *publicare*, to make public. It is not without reward, and it is not without risk. Today, it is becoming less of an option and more of an expectation, whilst at the same time the competition is increasing, and the standards are rising. Fortunately, the process is well understood and can be managed.

There remain, however, as many good reasons not to publish as there are to publish. When I run workshops on getting published, I always make sure people in the audience tell me all the reasons they know not to publish as well as the reasons they should. That is because it is often more useful to discover why we do not do things we want to do than it is to nag ourselves with all the reasons we should. One approach makes us feel guilty and apathetic while the other may help remove the obstacles and spur us into action.

Fear

Fear is the most common reason people give for not publishing. There may be many more excuses, but when they really clear their throats and decide to be honest, it is fear that they admit to. Every time I ask people at workshops why they don't publish, they answer with all sorts of compelling reasons, such as those I review below, before finally adding 'and fear'. That admission is guaranteed to generate a ripple of nervous laughter throughout participants. Although it may be one of the last reasons we are prepared to admit, it is almost always the most powerful. This is reasonable! Your research is important to you; it means something. You do not want to put yourself in a position where someone might dismiss it.

What if people laugh? What if they say that all the work we feel so good about is actually completely off-base? What if someone has done it all before?

Everyone has fears about all sorts of things, and some of the fears we have are ancestral and useful. A rush of fear if we are alone in a dark house and hear someone moving around downstairs is useful, but it is not so good if the house is silent, we have never yet met a burglar, we have locked all our doors and yet we still lie awake night after night worrying.

A field in psychology called cognitive behaviour explores how people convert thought to emotion and back again. Therapists try to help people distinguish between irrational thoughts creating inappropriate emotions from rational thoughts which reflect a more balanced view of the issue. The objective is to test the thoughts that are creating the emotion, giving them a 'reality check'. What lies behind the fear people have about 'getting published'? Can we subject these fears to a reality check?

There is a simple exercise you can apply to test your own fears. On a sheet of paper, note the precise thought you have when the fear of publishing sweeps over you. Is it that you are a bad writer? Is it that you think people will dismiss your work outright? Is it perhaps a fear that they will criticize it for being shallow? Or that maybe they will steal your ideas and claim them as their own? Now, how strongly do you believe these thoughts right now? One hundred per cent? Seventy? Write it down.

Recording your fears is a positive step in your own publishing development. It means you are no longer procrastinating meekly but are actually taking steps to overcome the most significant inhibitors facing new authors – fear. Make sure you use the opportunity to commit all your fears to paper, however foolish they may seem. Someday, when you feel like sharing them, you may be surprised to see how many of them appear on other people's lists.

The next step is to examine each fear more carefully and subject it to analysis. Let's take a few of them and see how they might stand up to closer inspection.

'I can't write!'

How bad a writer can you be? You got through school and into university, didn't you? Have you ever managed to express yourself on a birthday card or in a love letter? Did the recipients understand the message? Of course, they did. Did you fail every essay or paper sent in for marking, on the grounds that they were incomprehensible? Of course, you did not.

So, what exactly is the problem? The word 'bad', at the very least, might be changed to 'mediocre' or 'inconsistent'. Is that what you must accept?
NO.

Perhaps writing does not come easily to you; perhaps you do not find the words miraculously flowing from your fingertips. That's okay. No one else does either, not even professional writers. There are only three attributes which separate good writers from mediocre writers:

- preparation
- practice
- patience

All of those are skills you can develop, and this book will show you how. Now, if you can see that your writing cannot be truly bad, but may need developing, and you can see that there are ways to develop it, what does that do to your fear?

Note again on your paper the key points that helped reduce your fear and make a note of how much you now believe your first statement, 'I can't write'. Twenty per cent? Ten per cent? Finally, note the action or actions you plan to take. We waste far too much time worrying about our fears.

'They'll dismiss my work outright!'

Will they? Why should they? Is it a poor piece of research? What do your colleagues say? How did your supervisor or client or sponsor like it?

In Chapter 4 we will see how to determine the real implications of your research. Authors often fail to describe them because they have not seen them themselves. For now, examine as you did in the first question exactly why you are afraid. Once again, subject this fear to analysis. Are people in your field really confident that they know it all? Would they not read with interest another person's contribution? Didn't your supervisor say it was good, and haven't they seen many more before yours? Haven't your colleagues supported you? The answer to all these questions is likely to be 'yes', for even a reasonable piece of work. That it may not change the world is not the point right now. If it helps people to look at it a little differently, that can be enough.

If your piece of research really is substandard, or if your new conceptual framework has actually not grown beyond the rough sketch stage, you may be better off not publishing right now. You must, however, test that assumption thoroughly with trusted colleagues, because you may be underestimating your own work. That is very different from publishing, say, a paper about a common error you made in your research, from which you are learning and which you are willing to share with others.

One of the benefits of electronic publishing is that you can receive prompt feedback from other people, most of whom you have never met. If you are still nervous about the quality of your research, consider submitting a short note to one of the electronic journals or conferences available on the internet. It is likely that you will receive at least some response about your piece. Internet *fora* are good places to test and share ideas. You may find another researcher on the other side of the world interested in your work.

Finally, remember that learning from criticism is one of the arts of academic life. Everyone learns to use critical reasoning powers, and therefore it would be unusual for someone not to look on your work critically, as you look on the work of others. But that does not mean they will reject it outright, although it does mean they might, even should, evaluate it critically. Would you expect any less of your peers or your students? We know from our own experience of evaluating research that we are not criticizing the person when we criticize the work. We can therefore rest assured that criticism of our own work will be fully in the spirit of academic enquiry. If we have done all the right preparation and have passed the final review stages, we do not need to fear that anyone will dismiss our work at a glance.

Review now how strongly you believe your original statement that people will reject your work outright. It probably is not a reasonable fear, once you think about it. What is it worth – 10 per cent? What is your plan of action to further reassure yourself?

'People will steal my ideas'

As we saw earlier, this fear forms part of the 'publish as you go' debate. Fear of theft by unscrupulous ideas burglars can probably be left to disturb the sleep of a scientist who is about to discover the cure for cancer and therefore stands to gain riches and international prestige in the process. For the rest of us, we can generally assume that other people are busy working out their own ideas and, however brilliant and original we think our ideas are, they think theirs are, too.

We reviewed earlier the idea of concurrent publishing as an integral part of many people's publications strategy. As long as you present a paper at a conference or discuss your thoughts in a discussion group, you are publicizing your ideas. At least by publishing them you can lay claim to them and increase the possibility that anyone who refers to your ideas or research will at least credit you accordingly.

It seems that the real issue is the matter of attaching one's name to the research findings. With a clear strategy worked out, which we will explore in later chapters, you do not have to fear that people will not credit you for your work. After all, we know exactly who discovered the three laws of motion, who created the law of relativity, where the term 'pasteurized' comes from and the name of the man who first mass-produced cars.

'I don't know where to start!'

This fear relates to one of our oldest and most primitive – the fear of the dark. How can we push ourselves into an abyss, into a huge gaping black hole called 'publishing' when we do not know enough about it? How will we know that our papers will stand up to the scrutiny of the editor and his or her review board? How will we even know to which journal to send it? How will we start to write? How long will it take? Will we ever finish it? Few people take pleasure in being lost. Publishing is a mysterious process, but it is one that anyone can understand, learn, and master.

This is the central thesis of this book, but it is not your only source of help. Attending writers' workshops, meeting colleagues who have published, and talking to people who edit and review journals will help demystify the publishing business and help you write the kind of papers which will eventually be published. For now, the answers to the following questions are brief:

- *How can I push myself into an abyss...?* You will not do that. The first rule of a successful publishing strategy is to do your homework. Most papers fail because the writer has not considered the needs of the journal and its readers. The following chapters will show you how.
- *How will I know that my papers will stand up to the scrutiny of the editor and review board?* By following the straightforward guidance of reviewers, editors, and other authors, either by contacting them directly, or learning from their ideas distilled in the pages of this book.
- *How will I start?* By thinking through a few main points discussed later, concentrating on purpose, implications, and the right target journal.
- *How long will it take?* To do what? To write before undertaking the initial preparatory stage? A few months, maybe years, possibly forever. After spending some directed preparation time and then writing? A few days.
- *Will it ever be finished?* The paper, yes. The ongoing quest for perfection, no.

The need for perfection

Recall the advice of the doctoral supervisor quoted earlier: 'There are only two types of articles; those that are perfect and never get published, and those that are good enough and do.'

The need to be perfect inhibits many people who do not put their words to paper. There is always one more edit that will make it right, always one more piece of information, always one more question to answer. But how can you create perfection if you do not create at all? All any of us can do is our best. 'Best' includes being aware of the sell-by date. The perfect article may indeed be perfect, two years after everyone else in the field has moved on. It might be so perfect that you can frame it page by page in your study.

Indeed, why not think of other ornaments you can make with the pages of unfinished, nearly perfect articles? As we saw earlier, the competition in this market is fierce. As you are patiently perfecting your article, there will probably be two or three people submitting a paper similar to you. They will be published in six months while you are still chasing another reference.

What's the worst that can happen?

What if, with all your best efforts behind you, your paper is returned to you, either asking for revisions or informing you politely that it is simply not acceptable at all? Even the best authors have been rejected. If that is the worst that happens, is it really so bad?

There's always the possibility that another journal might accept a version of what the first has rejected, not because its standards are lower, but because the needs at the time are different. And even if every journal rejects it, what does this really tell you? At worst it means you need to do some more work on the topic. That is no problem. After all, that is your job: researching and contributing to the body of knowledge. Just as not all of your students will get an 'A', so not all of your papers will hit the mark.

More likely, if you have done your homework, you will be asked to revise your paper before it can be accepted for publication. We will discuss this in more detail later, but the most important point is never to forget that the comments from an editorial review are free, honest, and of high quality. Welcome the opportunity to revise as a learning experience; it is a positive activity, not one to fear or be embarrassed about.

Priorities

'I'm too busy!' you say. Of course, you are. And so are the authors who are being published right now in your field. If being published is important to you, you will find the time. But first, consider what you mean by time. Is it time spent nervously staring at the screen, going nowhere? Or time, maybe an hour each day, putting your thoughts on paper and organizing your approach?

The Performance Group in Oslo (Bjelland et al. 1994) studied similarities amongst those described as peak performers – writers, musicians, politicians, academics, and industrialists. Amongst their several shared characteristics was their ability to concentrate intensely on whatever they were doing.

They quoted the then Nokia Chief Executive Jorma Ollila saying: 'If someone focuses on what they are doing, they can do in 15 minutes what would otherwise take them four hours.'

Taking time to write necessarily means taking significant blocks of time, but it is more important to manage the quality of the time rather than the quantity. Successful, prolific authors are probably as busy as, or busier than, you are. They may only block out one hour every two days to work on their manuscript, but in that time they are able to concentrate on what they are doing. The question, therefore, is not 'How much time do I have?' but 'How can I use the time I have most effectively?'

The better time management courses do not simply teach about what emails to open and how to delegate. They teach about knowing what your priorities are and how to get on with them. If the project matters to you, you will find the time.

Summary

This chapter has drawn together some of the most common reasons people give for why they should, or should not, publish. Each point has a flip side: the benefits of people knowing about your work does open up the possibility that they may not approve of it. This, as we have seen earlier, is the nature of learned debate and not something to take personally.

Each of us has different incentives in mind and experience different constraints. Before going much further, you might like to note your own reasons for publishing and all the reasons which have prevented you so far. It is then a matter of concentrating on the benefits and seeing how you can minimize the risks. After all, people who have no fear are not brave, they are fearless. Bravery is having the fear but doing it anyway.

As publishing and funding are so inter-related, the next chapter will review key principles and obstacles to getting funded.

Action points

Each chapter in this book will conclude with a task which will help you shape your ideas for publication. You can do it right now or, if you want to read on further, do it later. But do it soon, even if you revise and change it later on. Use a notebook, or make a file on your PC, to keep the notes you make. When taken together they will create a plan for you to work through every time you write an article for publication.

First, write a list of five to ten benefits to you of becoming published. Benefits are things that mean something to you. They might be personal benefits, such as: 'I would like to see my name in a well-respected journal', or they might be professional benefits such as 'Writing an article about my research will expose it to others and might bring me speaking engagements or consultancy work.' Consider the benefits to your organization, such as how getting an article published will increase your research ratings or appease your head of department or publicize the good work you have been doing. You might choose career benefits: 'I need to be able to list some good publications on my CV before I make my next job application' or any other kind of relevant benefits.

These are your objectives, the end-products of becoming published, the reasons you will make the time to craft your ideas into some well-chosen words. Review them now and again and change or add to them.

Next, note any excuses you used for not turning your ideas into publishable articles. List no more than six and, for each one, note your feelings then think of a counterargument that you really believe, a conclusion about the barriers and the counterargument, and the action you can take to break through any fears you might have. For example:

- I can talk about my ideas, but I become stuck when I try to write them down (*thought*).
- That makes me feel worried about exposing something I've written to an audience (*feeling*).
- But the paper I discussed at the graduate seminar was well received (*counterargument*).
- I can express my ideas if I care about something and think carefully about my audience (*conclusion*).
- I need to start with something I'm really interested in, that will be of benefit to me, and consider carefully who will be reading it (*action*).

Reference

Bjelland, Dahl and Partners (1994). *The Keys to Breakthrough Performance.* Oslo: Performance Group.

3 WHY LOOK FOR RESEARCH FUNDING?

Introduction

Research includes a broad range of activities. As discussed in this book's opening chapter, the twin activities of publishing and funding are often inseparable and together create successful career paths. Many governments and funders combine the notion of dissemination (usually through publications) in their definitions of research.

As briefly discussed in Chapter 1, and returned to again in Chapter 5, moves towards open access increasingly place the costs of publishing on individual academics. This is because publishers will agree to immediate open access to papers only if a fee is paid. Funded researchers build this fee into their research budgets. Other, non-funded, academics are expected to pay individual author submission fees. One consequence is that authors who are neither funded nor can afford author submission fees are increasingly denied access to places to publish. Another consequence is that the pressure to receive research funding increases as academics realize that this is, increasingly, the only way their research papers can be published.

For further discussion, see, for example, Paige Mann (2022) Chapter 5 in this volume.

What is research?

It may seem like an obvious question, but it is worth clarifying what research means in a funding and publishing context. This is reviewed in more detail in the next chapter through an exploration of what is 'good' research. Here, it is worth reminding ourselves of the key impetus behind doing research: research is what you do when you do not know what to do. Research is a process of finding an answer, solving a problem, or illuminating an issue, a people, or a practice, for example. At its heart, therefore, is uncertainty. If you knew the answer you would not have to find out. People who seek

DOI: 10.4324/9781003259718-4

research funding typically want the support, monetary and more, of a partner who appreciates the uncertainty, the risk, and sometimes the worry of delving into new areas or questions.

That is why it is important to understand how research funding may help academics achieve a wider range of outputs than would be possible with less collaboration or funding. Each funder offers guidance about what kinds of outputs are expected and point out that these will differ by programme. Although I return to the subject of criteria in later chapters, I want to provide here a long example which shows how a funder structures its opportunities to reflect its ethos and also provide support for high-risk projects.

For example, in the United States (New Interdisciplinary Projects in the Social Sciences 2021) the Social Science Research Council funds research for inter-disciplinary working groups that are innovative in their research questions, frameworks, and methods, leading to new and innovative answers. As explained on its website, the projects it funds usually involve risk, they also potentially lead to high rewards. The umbrella programme involves research teams of different backgrounds, disciplines, and institutions seeking dialogue and collaboration. The aim of the programme is to produce what the Council envisages as 'creative' scholarship that can address both new and 'enduring' questions, issues, or debates. It also expects the projects it funds to build links within the social sciences and create new connections between social science, natural sciences, and the humanities. The programme's emphasis on collaboration and inter-disciplinary work is embedded throughout the programme's criteria and its funding opportunities: the amount and type of funding ($50,000) the programme offers working groups reflect those broad objectives, as they contribute to direct costs required for meetings, travel, accommodations, meals, or research assistance.

Eligibility and criteria for team composition reflects an ethos and expectation of partnership. For example, the lead Principal Investigator must be on the faculty of those institutions already recognized by the SSRC as partners in the College and University Fund for the Social Sciences (CUF) (a consortium of higher education institutions (HEIs) and funders). Other participants in the working group, however, may be from institutions outside the CUF, and the Call specifically notes that a preference will be given to teams with leadership from different institutions. Further, the Call adds that the SSRC 'strongly encourages collaborations that include faculty from minority-serving institutions'. The criteria also specify that working groups should be led by people from at least two different disciplines.

It would therefore be surprising, and a waste of everyone's time, if applicants failed to adhere to not only the technical criteria imposed but, importantly, to the ethos that underpins the creation of the research team. Reviewers would, for example, expect to see in any proposal statements affirming and reinforcing the points described above. Indeed, in its instructions on how to apply, the funder explicitly states that applicants should make clear the transformative potential of the funding for the long-term impact of the project as well as the rationale behind the proposed group of participants. They also want to have considerable detail (250 words each) about the Principal Investigators and Co-Investigators, and information about the disciplinary background and expertise of those who are likely to be participants. The criteria form part not only of the proposal assessment but also the characteristics of those making the decisions about funding. The review committee is composed of scholars from a variety of backgrounds and whose type of work 'represents the type of border-crossing approaches' that is being sought. The four criteria used to assess projects show, again, how the participants themselves are an integral part of the evaluation process which will assess the: 'contribution to the social sciences, networks and participants, project design, and potential contribution to social science in the public interest'.

By this stage in the process of assessing the Programme's ethos and criteria it should therefore come as no surprise that the Call points out that the funder will scrutinize applications not simply on the 'usual standards of rigorous academic inquiry' but also on how innovative the groups of scholars are participating. This is notable and instructive, as some academics may assume that proposals are only assessed on their scientific merit. Here, not only is the diversity of working groups important, but also is the way that the proposal shows how the project will 'pursue the application of new methodologies or analytical frameworks or that combine existing approaches in novel ways'.

As I stressed at the beginning of this section, many research ideas involve bold, risky approaches. The above example shows that creating a funded project for the SSRC helps spread the risk inherent in novelty and uncertainty and, in many ways, reinforces their importance. It also shows that some projects can never be conceived as stand-alone entities. On large programmes, the concept of collaboration extends beyond the immediate project team to the programme as a whole. The themes and outputs can be spread across different projects as well as focusing on the overall programme. I will explore this in more detail in later chapters.

Creating and leading teams

Many new researchers are surprised that the success of their project will not depend so much on their personal skills and intelligence, but on how well they work with other people. In this section, I look at teams and networks to illustrate the nature of collaboration from the smallest project-based unit to university inter-departmental groups, to networks drawn from different regions or countries.

Even small research projects involve other people to some extent. An historian working on an archive project, a classicist involved in an international exchange, or four people from different European universities collaborating on policy issues, all need 'people skills'. It is therefore apparent that the ability to work well with other people is noted as a key skill. This becomes particularly apparent with larger projects which are often complex multi-disciplinary, multi-institution, multi-country entities. For many European Union funding programmes which are multi-institution and multi-country, for example, lead applicants without previous team management experience will be expected to accept a junior role in any prospective team. Only those with a previous international track record in leading multi-institution teams may consider themselves for the position of coordinator. Collaborating in teams will, therefore, be essential for new researchers, to enable them to be guided while gaining experience.

There is always a risk that a research team may fail to reach its goals due to a number of team-related issues. These may include differing expectations, role definition, and communication. In her experience as a researcher and team leader, one well-funded team leader told me that a common cause of project failure is that the team breaks down. This is usually, in her view, through lack of supervision. Too often, the team leader fails to lead by meeting the team regularly and helping resolve issues and challenges as they arise.

One of the most difficult adjustments for research leaders to make is to distance themselves from the immediate research process. Leading a team means letting go of the day-to-day business of research – the literature reviews, the interviews, the detailed data analysis, for example. The team leader's role is both one of project and intellectual leadership. From a project management viewpoint, the job appears quite technical. There are overall strategic goals, aims and objectives, broken into discrete areas of work with timetables, milestones and outcomes. The team leader is there to see not only that the separate parts of the project are proceeding to schedule and plan, but to anticipate and negotiate changes when, and sometimes before, those become necessary. Most importantly, the leader sees that the discrete parts work together in balance to contribute to the whole. Only a team leader with a helicopter view of the whole project will be able to see how the parts fit and move together. Doing that essential task is what removes the role of team leader from that of hands-on researcher. When I interviewed Prof.

Rosalind Edwards at South Bank University, she was directing a five-year ESRC-funded programme on Families and Social Capital. Team leadership was, she said, one of the most exciting and most difficult parts of her job. Directing a team of professors and researchers was vital to the success of the project, and bound to be interesting, invigorating, and challenging. At the time of our interview, she was leading the first ESRC programme at a 'new' university which added a layer, she told me, of enormous responsibility and privilege. Further, as a well-published feminist of some note and authority, she gained some satisfaction in at least the partial realization of a political goal to see more women in senior positions of both structure and power. While realizing that goal was satisfying, it was not without its disappointments. When she created the team for the ESRC proposal, for example, she knew that she had to make tough decisions about who would belong and who would not belong. This contravened some of her feminist ethics about inclusivity but was necessary to create a balanced team. It was also necessary to remove herself from the nitty-gritty of research, she told me:

> I often feel uneasy when I listen to the other researchers in the team meetings talk about their work. Part of me wants to be doing the interviews myself, to be interpreting that data.

The role of a team leader will include:

- Targeting the appropriate funder or responding to a request for a proposal.
- Researching the suitability of the funder before submitting a proposal.
- Selecting the appropriate team.
- Creating the budget.
- Writing the proposal.
- Meeting the potential funder and making presentations when appropriate.
- Finalizing the agreement.
- Working with the team to set schedules.
- Meeting regularly with team members to explore progress.
- Leading academic debates within the group to maintain intellectual rigour.
- Ensuring the project adheres to budget.
- Negotiating changes when necessary with the team and funder.
- Reporting to the funder when appropriate.
- Creating the final report and participating in feedback mechanisms.

- Overseeing creation, and sometimes leading as author, on related papers and other publications.
- Helping the team reflect on its learning.

The evident ability to work well with others is therefore a key skill sought by many funders of research. This is because, in anything other than small-scale projects, research is a collaborative effort – collaboration amongst a research team; collaboration with the 'client' team at the funding institution; and possibly collaboration across different disciplines or institutions.

Research teams do not just succeed through the momentum of a project, or through the individual brilliance of their members. A good team needs skilled leadership, to manage a range of issues from motivation to work division to deadline adherence to reflection on learning from the project.

Many businesses – but few universities – use psychographic profile instruments to help select 'balanced' teams. Probably the best-known and most widely used of these instruments is the Myers–Briggs Type Indicator, MBTI, based on the personality theories and research of Carl Jung. The MBTI and other psychographic profile instruments help identify areas of work preference, which can give insights into how people can work effectively together.

Deciding what to research

In a review of UK research funding Paul Nurse (Nurse, 2015, 3) summarized the importance of deciding what to research, emphasizing the decision-making process:

> Making good decisions about what research topics and which researchers should be supported is an integral part of the research process and is crucial for a successful cost-effective research endeavour. This requires proper investment in good quality decision making, and should not be seen as an administrative burden, but rather an essential part of the research process, as well as a mechanism to ensuring that research funds are spent wisely and not wasted on inappropriate research.

That quote is well worth remembering, particularly when those of us anxious to complete and submit a research proposal feel delayed by internal review processes. The point of such processes, whether managed by a central or departmental process (or both), is to ensure that decisions about choosing a research topic are both clear and transparent.

It may be useful at this point to review briefly what we mean by the research process. Any piece of research is built around a design, which begins with identifying a problem and then explores the issue that guides our understanding. The research problem is the specific question being examined by the researcher, such as 'can the culture of the public service adapt to performance reward techniques?'. The problem might arise from background to the research, such as previous researchers' flaws or superficialities, or it might arise from a specific question being imposed by a research client who is funding institutional research.

As most researchers know, problem definition is one of the most difficult stages of any research project. Some people carry on with inadequate problem identification and then face the difficulty of trying to redefine it midway through the project or even afterwards. If they still have not defined it properly by the time they write their paper or submit their proposal, they are unlikely to please a reviewer who is left scratching their head and wondering what the fuss is about. The applicant must therefore attend to the implications of both the problem and the issue, where relevant. We explore the nature and importance of 'implications' in later chapters.

That does not mean that all research requires funding: not everyone needs or wants research funding. Although most academics regard part of their jobs as including both research and teaching, the research component of their job description may be, for many, adequate as it is. At the barest minimum, it means keeping current in their field while for others it is a requirement of their institution that they are engaged in research as a condition of their employment.

A professor who is expected to spend, say, a third of their time on 'scholarship' may be able and willing to conduct that research relatively independently, perhaps only depending on a departmental administrators and research students for support and resource. Many people only need and prefer this arrangement. Once they move towards gaining research funding, however, several features of their work will change dramatically because there are some projects that can only be accomplished with extra resources of time, people, equipment, or software. Those cost money, and most would exceed a standard departmental budget.

For example, two researchers at the University of East Anglia, Prof. Arjan Verschoor and Prof. Ben D'Exelle, worked for two decades to improve farming in Uganda. They set out to explore how the three million smallholder farmers perceive risk. Why was that important? Why would risk profile affect farming? For the researchers, it was central to the aim of improving farming in the region. They hypothesized that the ways in which smallholder farmers in eastern Uganda perceived financial risks may influence their decisions about investing in productivity-boosting technologies such as fertilizer, seeds, and irrigation. During two decades of research, they found that farmers did not, and with good cause, trust existing insurance policies. That was because, the researchers learned, the insurers only paid out after a drought had occurred – which tended to happen every six years or so – and sometimes did not pay at all. This had an important impact on livelihoods and food security, as the researchers knew, mainly because farmers were reluctant to take out loans to improve their farming practices because they were then risking not being able to repay the loans.

Through their multi-sited (and more about that later) research with farmers, government departments, banks, and international aid organizations the researchers were able to devise a unique Uganda Agriculture Insurance Scheme (UAIS) in 2016 which subsidizes insurance as well as provides good quality seeds and other services. The methods the researchers devised have improved farming practices and food security in Uganda and also had a wider impact worldwide. As Prof. Verschoor explained (UK Research and Innovation 2021) more than 1.5 billion people in the developing world live in poor smallholder farming households fearful of uninsured risk: 'Our research shows how insurance can be designed to help farmers better cope with risk, so that they can confidently invest in their farms, increase productivity and help bring about food security'.

The example also shows how, sometimes, research success relies on collaboration with others outside one's own institution. Indeed, a desire for inter-institutional collaboration drives an ethos behind research funding. In his review of UK research councils, Paul Nurse (Nurse, 2015, 3) stressed that:

> The most effective research systems at producing knowledge for the public good are characterised by freedom of action and movement: they need to be permeable and fluid, allowing the ready transfer of ideas, skills and people in all directions between the different sectors, research disciplines, and various parts of the research endeavour. Artificial barriers which reduce permeability or mutual respect between the different parts of the system should be resisted as they reduce the effectiveness of the research system – both to produce knowledge and for the effective use of that knowledge for applications. Research systems thrive on excellent research scientists who are strongly motivated most often by great curiosity and by the freedom to pursue their intellectual interests, and who make a difference to our understanding of the world – whether

from a within a single discipline, or in collaboration with others who can bring different disciplinary perspectives to bear on complex problems.

Another good example of such collaborative, inter-disciplinary research is the ESRC-funded 'A National Observatory of Children's Play Experiences During COVID-19'. This ran from November 2020 to January 2022 amongst researchers from three different groups: the UCL Institute of Education, the School of Education at the University of Sheffield, and The Bartlett Centre for Advanced Spatial Analysis at UCL.

The research context was the coronavirus pandemic. The researchers knew that the pandemic had significantly affected where, how, and with whom children and young people were able to socialize. They wanted to know more about how such practices of socializing, particularly play and games, had or had not changed during the pandemic. They devised specific research questions, which I include here because they are exemplary in situating clearly the questions within the lived, empirical, practical environment as well as the more theoretical (University of Sheffield, 2020):

- How have children and young people been playing during the pandemic, from the outbreak of the virus, through lockdowns and school closures, and during ongoing social distancing?
- How has the COVID-19 pandemic featured in play and expressive culture (including language, humour, festivals and rituals, beliefs, stories, and making) and what insights does this give into children's unique experiences of it?
- How does this play and culture compare with that of the past, and between different communities?
- How can different scholarly approaches (such as history, folklore, multimodality, education and cultural studies) help us better understand the significance of play and expressive culture for well-being during times of crisis, struggle and change?

Their methods included conducting an online survey and asking people and adults to share examples of play through artefacts such as photos, drawings, sound recordings, and video clips. These were then captured and to be made available to the general public through the project's 'Play Observatory'.

The researchers were clear about the outcomes of the project, including a searchable online collection of examples and media that would be permanently available for future scholars from the British Library. This means that a major concern of funders was met – the results were available for further research by those outside the immediate project team. More publicly available outputs were also designed into the project, again meeting the funding criterion of public dissemination (particularly when public, taxpayers' money is being spent), with an online exhibition at the V&A Museum of Childhood. Another significant output was a toolkit co-designed with staff from Great Ormond Street Hospital. This can be used for those wanting to understand the importance of play and how to support it, particularly during uncertain and stressful periods.

Another way of 'changing the world' is to be specific about who is the ideal funder. This means being aware of your research environment and context. For example, there are non-academic charities and other organizations set up to specifically improve people's lives through action and policy. These may be the ideal funders for those directing their research at societal change.

For example, the abrdn Financial Fairness Trust was established from previous incarnations related to the multinational insurance company Standard Life. They changed their name to better reflect their mission and goals to 'contribute towards strategic change which improves financial well-being in the UK. We want everyone to have a decent standard of living and have more control over their finances'. Those aims are fulfilled by funding research, campaigns, and policies 'improve the living standards and personal finances of people struggling to make ends meet' (Financial Fairness Trust 2022).

For academics thinking of applying for funding, the information on their website is clear, as is the context. They describe how society has changed, with a shift towards more individual than state responsibility for financial management and protection. Further, they note how the current national context in the UK has increased the urgency people feel towards finances and well-being, with the cost-of-living increases and damages wrought by the global pandemic. Their website also provides more information about the trust's history, the way it is governed and its publications. I will return to this example in future chapters, discussing how to target the right funder. For now, the important point is that there are some funders who are specially created to effect change, not just think or write about it. Those are the people with whom a funding relationship can help deliver the kinds of changes researchers may also be working towards.

It is critically important for such funders to be clear about the context, whether that is expressed in a short literature review or other overview of context. If a literature review is appropriate for a funding proposal, it is there to demonstrate to the funder that there is a gap, or an error, that needs attention.

Researchers often struggle with the issue of a 'literature review', asking how to approach it. The main consideration is to remember that the literature is just what has gone before. It is work that has touched on the issue you want to research. The question now is, has any of that literature actually helped resolve the issue or problem? If so, what gaps may remain? If not, what need to be done? The survey of the literature for an academic paper or proposal is the critical point where we answer those questions for the reader and tell them how so far the problem or issue may have been framed or illuminated, but more needs to be done. This, you are saying, is not enough. Those other scholars have done a good job so far, but all their research so far does not get us where we need to be.

It is also the point at which you are demonstrating to the funder that you know what needs to be done, that you are an expert and up to date in your field. That may be the most important consideration for the funder. As one trustee of a charity remarked to me about a proposal they did not fund: 'One we didn't fund was on childcare trusts. What were the researchers going to say that we didn't know already? We already knew it, so why fund it?'

For the same reason, many proposals which suggest specific research is necessary to change government policy also go unfunded. As a funder commented: 'what we want to see is whether these arguments are actually going to get anywhere. The researchers should know the answer to that. If you're trying to influence social policy, you have to know the social policy context'.

Against the odds

As I reviewed in the first chapter, public research money is not, according to many researchers, distributed fairly amongst HEIs. Those which score highest on the UK's Research Excellence Framework (REF) receive more funding than those who do not. Many people are critical of this approach, arguing that new universities or those without a record of accomplishment in research can never break through into the 'elite' arena. A problem related to funding parity is that historically fewer applications to research councils are made from modern universities, reinforcing the systematic disadvantage theory and supporting the notion that if academics at modern universities had the same amount of time to work on proposals as their colleagues in the older sector, they would be able to submit as many proposals. Another disadvantage may arise from a differential in infrastructure where more established universities can support the kind of research into science and engineering that elude newer, less resource-rich universities.

That is why, with the emphasis on central funding being linked to the REF, newer, modern universities may get less when compared to the older, more established, more research-intensive universities. The kind of research most often done in the modern universities has traditionally been more practical, applied, and professionally related than in the older universities. Much of it is funded by outside agencies, such as industry or local government, and due to restrictions on intellectual property, some of that does not get published in peer review journals. This then affects what is deemed by external assessors to be first-class, internationally respected research. As I outlined in Chapter 1, published research, particularly in journals, affects institutional reputation and funding success which, in turn, affects further publications, research, and institutional reputation.

The situation may, however, be changing. Recent studies about research funding show that while the new universities were less successful in winning research funding than the older universities, the gap was not as big as might have been expected. This likely indicates that the quality of applications from the modern universities is high.

Gender issues and research

Another disparity in research funding relates to gender, where it seems that research money is not, distributed fairly amongst men and women. One reason may relate to seniority disparity. To apply for most research projects, the principal applicant must be a senior member of the academic staff. This requirement reveals a number of related issues, notably that of gender bias.

A study by the National Centre for Social Research, commissioned by the Wellcome Trust and six research councils, enquired into why men win research funding more often than women do. The summary report by the Wellcome Trust (Blake and La Valle 2000) said:

> The awarding of research grants is at the very heart of the academic system. As research funders we know how many applications we receive a year and how many of those applications are successful. We also know that, in the UK, once an application is received there is no evidence of gender discrimination – men and women have similar award rates and this observation is consistent across a range of funding organisations. Yet, in reaching this conclusion it became apparent that gender may be a determinant of grant application behaviour – women, in general, were applying for fewer research grants than men.

The study concluded that there was, indeed, a gender bias, but not one in the funding agencies themselves. The gender bias in funding is rooted within the structure of academe itself. The Trust continued:

The findings from the study indicate that many factors influence grant application behaviour. The survey results show that women were as successful as men in getting the grants they applied for but were less likely to apply for grants because of their status in the institution and the support they received. The main influences on grant application behaviour were seniority, employment status, tenure, type of institution, professional profile, institutional support, career breaks and family circumstances. Whilst many factors affect both men and women, some disproportionately deter women from making applications. For example, criteria designed by research funders to help define who can apply for research funding can produce a gender bias at the application stage, because more women than men are employed on fixed-term contracts and are at lower academic grades.

Women are still under-represented within the senior academic tiers. This, the study concluded, explains why more men apply than women do and why, consequently, men win most funding. Although it was outside the scope of that report, it may be reasonable to extrapolate that other people not represented in the senior echelons will, too, be under-represented in both applications and awards: people of colour, for example, people with disabilities, people from different socio-economic backgrounds.

For anyone who believes 'the personal is political', this may be one very good reason to apply for research funding. Recommendations from the report urged funding bodies to review their policies to widen the criteria for application. Women, and potentially others who see a structural bias in academe, are encouraged to make statements within their funding applications about their particular circumstances.

Funded outputs

From scholarly borderlands above: *Expected Outputs*

While most funded projects produce scholarly journal articles and other publications, these need not be the sole projected products of these collaborations. The SSRC programme described above, for example, specified that they are especially interested in projects that broaden reach or impact. These might include creating new pedagogical resources or methodological toolkits that allow researchers to approach complex research questions, and also might include producing more public-facing publications and reports.

Another reason some scholars look for research funding is that they anticipate the benefits of what may precede and result from the core research.

I have reviewed some excellent research proposals that support their claims to benefit wider academic and non-academic audiences by building such engagement at the beginning.

Several years ago, George Marcus (1995) proposed that much research would benefit from being mobile and multi-sited. He was referring to projects that demanded that the researcher move around to understand what was occurring. Such projects might include, for example, research into movements of international aid, from the starting point of an agency based in Geneva conceiving an aid project, through to the agency acquiring resources for the aid, to providing the aid through project partners on the ground in, perhaps, Yemen. Other projects may include movements of organs for transplants, drugs for a global vaccination programme, wheat moving through a global supply chain, or international activism against animal testing. What would be required, obviously, is money to support the research in multiple locations, but perhaps less obviously is the need to incorporate the ideas and experiences of a wide range of social actors: government workers, banking executives, hospital personnel, border police, and so on. Researchers might therefore create on-site meetings, in-country planning exercises, end-user consultations. As Simon Coleman and Pauline van Hellerman (2011) wrote, to understand the perspective of people from different points in the network being researched means those perspectives and voices need to be brought in at the beginning of the project during the finer points of its design.

Just as the excerpt from the SSRC above indicated, the result of much research is disseminated through interesting and innovative ways. Of course, as discussed throughout this book, the necessary output is usually a peer-reviewed journal paper – but what sort of paper and where will it be discussed? Most authors appreciate feedback about their work, and a funded project may allow for the final results to be communicated at, for example, a specially convened workshop or a panel at an international conference. For projects with several collaborators, funding may allow participation in a range of conferences or events that would not be feasible otherwise.

Funding may also allow dissemination through public engagement not otherwise affordable. These activities may include performances, exhibitions, books, educational resources and other, sometimes expensive, means of communicating to a non-expert audience.

We will review more about public engagement and other dissemination opportunities in future chapters, but for now, think about funding as something that affects not just what you may consider to be the core research, but the results of the research as well.

Summary

There are many good reasons to apply for research funding, and some good reasons not to. What is required is a particular mindset that recognizes that the hard work and disappointments that characterize the struggle for funding are rewarded not by a single payment, but by a partnership. Extending the marriage metaphor introduced earlier, the marriage of interests should not merely be a marriage of convenience built mainly on material value. The most successful funding relationships prosper because each partner is genuinely interested in the other. The reason they stay together is not that they have to, but that they want to.

Hard work is expected on both sides. It is hard work, but winning research funding is only the first step in a relationship which has risks and opportunities for both partners. Although it may appear that only the researcher makes the effort to accommodate different styles and expectations, the reality is different. Researchers influence the relationship and the funder.

For researchers, exerting that influence may be a matter of political as well as personal ambition. The current status quo does not reflect the needs and circumstances of many who are systemically disadvantaged – new universities, emerging departments and disciplines, and individuals under-represented by virtue of their colour, gender, or disabilities. It is, therefore, important that a wide range of people apply for and win research funds.

The research landscape undoubtedly, will change. It will change when funders receive more innovative and well-constructed applications, and more applications in particular from people who are systemically disadvantaged. It will change as funders broaden their review committees and their choice of topics to increase diversity and equality.

Action points

1. It can be useful at this stage, before beginning the process of targeting the right funder, to list the pros and cons of what being funded means to you.
2. An important part of most funding applications is the extent to which they demonstrate collaboration. Are you sure about the ways you can, and want, to collaborate? Make a list of the aspects of your proposal idea that demand or can be enhanced by collaboration.
3. With whom and how will you collaborate? Taking the list from the S point above, sketch out the disciplines, regions, methodological opportunities and, if possible, the individuals with whom you might collaborate.

References

Blake, Margaret and Ivana La Valle (2000). *Who Applies for Research Funding? Key Factors Shaping Funding Application Behavior among Women and Men in British Higher Education Institutions.* Wellcome Trust and National Centre for Social Research. Available at: https://wellcome.org/sites/default/files/wtd003209_0.pdf

Coleman, Simon and Pauline von Hellermann (2011). 'Introduction: Queries, collaborations, calibrations'. In *Multi-sited Ethnography: Problems and Possibilities in the Translocation of Research Methods*, eds. Simon Coleman and Pauline von Hellermann. New York: Routledge, pp. 1–15.

Financial Fairness Trust (2022). *About.* Available at: https://www.financialfairness.org.uk/en/about

Nurse, Paul (2015). *Ensuring a Successful UK Research Endeavour: A Review of the UK Research Councils.* Available at: https://assets.publishing.service.gov.uk/government/uploads/system/uploads/attachment_data/file/478125/BIS-15-625-ensuring-a-successful-UK-research-endeavour.pdf

Social Science Research Council (2021). *New Interdisciplinary Projects in the Social Sciences.* Available at: www.ssrc.org/programs/college-and-university-fund-for-the-social-sciences/new-interdisciplinary-projects-in-the-social-sciences/

UK Research and Innovation (2021). 'Insuring previously uninsurable small farmers in Uganda'. Available at: https://www.ukri.org/about-us/research-outcomes-and-impact/esrc/insuring-previously-uninsurable-small-farmers-in-uganda/

University of Sheffield. (2020). *A National Observatory of Children's Play Experiences during COVID-19.* Available at: https://www.sheffield.ac.uk/education/research/childhood-and-youth/play-observatory-pandemic

4 WHAT IS GOOD RESEARCH?

Introduction

I recall the director of a large government funding agency remarking, somewhat drily, that considering how key the word 'research' is in the proposal title for 'research funding' he was surprised how little attention was paid to it. Indeed, as you apply for 'research funding' it is important to say exactly how you intend to carry out the research. But how will you know if it meets the assessors' standards? Or if it is any good? Method and other factors affecting 'good research' will arise indirectly as well as directly through funded projects and have implications for ethical, more diverse futures.

Earlier, I listed 10 'top tips', adding the important caveat that these are necessary but insufficient conditions for success. In this chapter, I want to explore and develop ideas about what makes for 'good research'.

Good research? The question is, I agree, loaded and normative. Is there a standard of 'good' research meaning, for example, appropriate and up to expectations, while also ethically sound? Whose expectations need to be met, and how will that view be formed? As with all assessments, it will be based on the opinion of the assessor. There is not one universal definition of good research: *what is good research is defined by those who assess it in particular instances.* The implication for researchers is, of course, to discover who the assessors are and how they reach their judgements.

More widely, however, my reading of the higher education landscape is that nowadays the trend has moved beyond ethics referring to mainly standard research design issues such as informed consent, to deeper, more difficult questions about who is involved, consulted, and valued. Academics may use a variety of techniques in studying their social worlds, including surveys, questionnaires, interviews, non-participant and participant observation, lived ethnography, multi-sited ethnography, discourse analysis, and photo elicitation. But why? And who decides?

DOI: 10.4324/9781003259718-5

This chapter will therefore review and explore 'good' in several ways and from different perspectives. The need is, I will argue, more urgent than ever. This book was originally written more than 20 years ago because there was a growing pressure to seek research funding, and those pressures have increased. This is a time of diminishing public funding and mixed attitudes towards public support of universities and research. The trend, undoubtedly, is towards gaining funding from other sources.

Some people are increasingly concerned that this move will affect the quality of research. Before we move on to the techniques of gaining and maintaining research relationships, we might consider the qualities of what people mean when they think of 'good research'. This chapter summarizes key points of a separate but related study undertaken specifically on the question of 'what is good research?' I concluded that while people may define 'good' and 'research' differently, when I interviewed a number of researchers and students about the question I reached a surprisingly high level of agreement, matching funders' and assessors' notions of what is 'good'. The qualitative judgements were aligned and will be discussed in more detail below.

What has become more obvious during the ensuring 20 years, however, is the extent to which people make value judgements of 'good' based on wider, ethical issues both in research's creation and dissemination. Another question I first explored was how people used research. Were there differences between how say, professors used research compared to students and might that therefore impinge on what they thought was 'good'? Is there a difference between how a researcher and funder uses research which may therefore affect their judgements? More recently, I have noticed that the ideas of collaboration, reflexivity, 'value' implications, research application, sharing, and utility have become more of the expectation about what is 'good'. Indeed, they have grown to form part of the definition of research itself, as will be discussed below.

What is good research?

Grounded and focused

I will begin with some of the ideas which emerged from my earlier study during the research for the first edition of this book. When I interviewed then an American Professor of Human Resource Management, I discovered that, in their case, good research was:

> Research which meets criteria of rigour, a systematic kind of modelling in its articulation and which ties back its process to a solid grounding

in what we know about the area that we're researching, so that there is a total integration of varying viewpoints in the grounding of the research design. Then in my mind for it to be good, it must then be very focused.

What struck me then, and resonates still, was the emphasis on 'grounding' and on focus. Good research, therefore, is situated within a knowledge base. The investigation of that knowledge, and its articulation and critique, forms an important part of every journal paper and funding paper. It may be described as 'literature review' or part of the 'context' – more of which I will discuss later. The point to stress here is that 'good' needs to be anchored to something within a discipline or discourse, particularly if your original idea, plan, or method aims to remedy or extend issues which have preceded you.

A British academic I interviewed made much the same point:

> For me, the challenge is to do research that is well-rooted in theoretical debates and conceptual discussion. Research can only be good if it stands on a firm footing. It has to be clear about the concepts.

Another British academic reflected a similar theme, saying that empirical disciplines must be tested empirically and theoretically. While there are many possible approaches, the right approach, she said, is determined by the research question:

> In recent years we've seen develop a multiplicity of research methods surveys and techniques to try to tease out meaning. Good qualitative research is consistent with the data, theoretically exciting, imaginative, and convincing. It is able to extend or develop or modify a theoretical notion that's around in a literature.

The need to use existing literature to set a context, and then to move to creating theory, is an important part of judging the impact, or 'so what?' factor in publishable research. More attention is paid to this in Chapter 7. Here, I want to draw attention to the above words about good research being both convincing and imaginative.

Marie Cornwall (2010), an experienced editor who has reviewed hundreds of papers and research notes, points offered tips for getting published, and paid particular attention to the criterion of being 'convincing'. When listing her top ten guidance points, she titled her section about qualitative research with the words 'convince me'. One of the first problems she encounters in reviewing qualitative research is that authors fail to fully describe the context for the social processes they are describing and analyzing. Where did the research take place? Where did the people they were studying live? Who were they? For institutions or geographical locations, detail must be provided, she continued, to give the reader insights into the characteristics of the place and the people who inhabit it, perhaps relating to the size of the population, the nature of the setting (urban, rural, suburban, for example), and other relevant details such as racial diversity (and, I would add, gender). There may arise concerns, I suggest, about revealing information that will identify people in a study where confidentiality and anonymity is key, but these may be ameliorated by fictionalizing to some extent those character-istics: I will return to this point in the next chapter about research ethics. What is important here is Cornwall's point that good research needs to be contextual and, to be publishable, that context needs to be articulated.

Another issue she raises is the trap authors may fall into relating to their claims about their data. This is particularly important when presenting quotes or referring to certain social interactions. Authors need to ensure they are clear about attributing meaning and understanding: are these the interpretations of the research participants, or the author? She stresses that this does not mean that simply reporting on what research participants do or say is sufficient:

> Qualitative research requires analysis on the part of the researcher; it is more than a report of respondents' views of social processes. When a qualitative paper remains at the descriptive level, with little analysis and even less abstraction to social phenomena or theory building, reviewers recommend a reject.

Another point she makes is relevant to those conducting quantitative re-search who also fail to convince reviews because they, too, remain at a de-scriptive and therefore unconvincing level. There is one aspect that she says often slips by reviewers, but an editor like her would not ignore: 'Too many author(s) focus on significance testing and the number of asterisks next to a coefficient; too few consider the size of the effect.' She urges others to be more specific about how much an effect matters, not simply its statistical effect. Once again, the importance of 'implications' or the 'so what' factor becomes clear.

Methodologically clear

Too often, experienced researchers take for granted that they know their method works, and they no longer spend sufficient time explaining it. Some people forget that applying for research funding necessarily entails describing in detail how exactly the research will be conducted. One funder remarked that inattention to method is often a clue that the applicant does not understand the funder's requirement; another funder said the problem may be one of complacency amongst experienced researchers:

> The problem for social science is that we've got such a range of possible ways of doing things, that you need to be quite experienced to set up a good research design and also know what you're talking about when it comes to method. I think an awful lot of people who are in senior positions, who tend to be the ones who apply for grants, are getting lazy about this. They're resting on their laurels.

As one British sociologist pointed out, that does not make it easy to evaluate compared to standard quantitative research:

> Quantitative research may be easier to evaluate, because it makes fewer claims: it's hypothetical and then deductive: either you do it well, such as designing questionnaires properly, which is fairly straightforward, or you don't.

Although that is a common perspective, people have developed methods to evaluate qualitative research based on what is having an impact. That it is a common perspective, however, bears thinking about when creating a funding proposal or a journal paper. How will you help the assessor evaluate your research? How does your choice of research method affect it?

Imaginative

Another British academic extends the concept of interdisciplinary and imaginative:

> It's empirically based. It uses current ideas and methods appropriately. It has a degree of imagination and creative thinking. It engages not only the person doing research, but those reading it. My orientation is applied. It needs to be accessible to all sorts of people. ... In my personal opinion, it's important to be inter-disciplinary.

And in a similar vein:

> Good research allows the reader to re-interpret the data. It rarely ends with an answer. The writing up needs to show transparency, honesty

and recognition of the limitations of what you did. The best research is self-reflective.

An MA student's definition is similar. She said:

> Good research would involve being part of the research situation. By that, I mean that research would not merely involve a god-like researcher applying his/her terms and categories to other people. Good research is dialogue.

The answers I found did not situate good research as so-called objective, standing outside the problem, trying to prove something. While good research seeks evidence, it also seeks to *engage* people. It is accessible to all sorts of people. The involvement of the reader, perhaps a reader who is not a scholar, is part of what makes it good. The researcher is part of the research itself.

Good research may also, in funders' terms, be described as research of 'high scientific merit', 'world-class', or 'research excellence'. As researchers Federico Ferretti et al. (2018, 731) noted, ideas of research excellence differ amongst academics, policy makers, and other bodies: 'When it comes to research policy, excellence is on top of the agenda. Yet, the meaning attributed to the notion of excellence differs markedly among both academics and policymakers alike.' Part of the reason that definition and understanding have become so important in recent years, they suggest, is because of the move towards funding research based on evidence. But, at the risk of slipping down another wormhole, what counts as 'evidence'? They also point out that describing research as excellent 'evokes a general sense of worth and, therewith, *shareability*' [italics theirs]. Further, as they note (Ferretti et al. 2018, 733): 'what counts as excellence is entertained by the imagination of some about what "excellent research" is; but what, political, social, and ethical commitments are built into the adopted notion and the choice of what needs to be quantified?' They conducted interview-based research with a range of participants and stakeholders, concluding that no single definition of 'excellence' was accepted by everyone and that no 'one size fits all' method of defining and measuring research could be adopted. They further concluded that the current trend to quantify excellence is likely to continue and called for more participation and transparency in the process.

Marie Cornwall (2010) points out that authors need to pay attention to claims about their data and what is required for publishable papers. Problems often arise in quantitative research about missing data, she explains, with authors often ignoring (or at least not discussing) the implications of missing data, especially when that affects the findings:

> Publishable papers should provide descriptive reports of the sample population in comparison to population characteristics such as age, education, and race. Publishable papers also include clear statements about how the loss of data, when using list-wise deletion, changes the characteristics of the sample.

Perhaps the most important conclusion, for readers here, is to recall that all definitions are contested, to note such variations in research proposals and papers, and to seek to understand the definitions and frameworks used, or even imposed, by specific funders and editors. There are related ethical and epistemological difficulties embedded in hidden power structures and values that deserve more space than available here. I turn to the subject of decentring, or decolonizing, research in the next chapter, following the urgent appeal of Linda Tuhiwai Smith (2012, 174–177) to ask:

> Whose research is it? Who owns it? Whose interests does it serve? Who will benefit from it? Who has designed its questions and framed its cope? Who will carry it out? Who will write it up? How will its results be disseminated?'

Flexible if necessary

Sometimes, things do not go according to plan. Such occurrences are not surprising for some forms of research that is necessarily innovative and exploratory. However well the design seemed at the outset, new developments, issues with accessibility, health, or other issues might make a change in direction necessary. Good research is research that accounts for these possibilities and makes changes that allow the research to continue to address the over-arching research question, aims, and objective. Funders are aware of such necessities and will usually accommodate changes, if the new approach is within the funded budget.

One significant example was the impact of COVID-19. The global pandemic offered new opportunities for researchers in many domains, but also had a negative impact on research underway that depended on access to people and equipment in buildings and other locations suddenly locked down, and research dependent on people for face-to-face interviews. Where possible, researchers often responded with effective adaptations, such as switching face-to-face interviews with those conducted online (and reflected on any positive or negative effects) or being able to postpone aspects of the research requiring travel. Funders, mainly, were understanding and collaborated with funded researchers to adapt. Advice on their website, for example, UK Research and Innovation (2022) was clear in their advice both for applying for extensions and, if necessary, changing the research method, particularly with regard to travel:

> Researchers, innovators and partners who are working internationally, or who need to travel, should follow the guidance from the relevant national and regional governments.

> You should switch to 'virtual' remote working, if possible.

The UK body composed of government-funded research councils, UKRI, also documented the impact of COVID-19 on researchers. Through a survey conducted in 2021, they found that (UK Research and Innovation 2021):

> 61% of researchers reported lockdown or shielding had negatively impacted their time for research; 58% reported that COVID-19 had made it impossible to do the research they planned; more than half reported that COVID-19 restrictions impacted other work activities, including teaching and administrative activities which reduced their time for research.

Nearly all researchers (88 percent), irrespective of gender, reported that increased childcare responsibilities impacted their research negatively. Nearly one-third, however, said that the pandemic had given them 'unexpected opportunities for their research' and more than half found the reduction in travel impacted positives on their time for research.

The impact on mental health for many, however, was grave, and in general both the benefits and drawbacks of COVID-19 were not distributed fairly: these issues will be discussed in more detail in the next chapter.

The government perspective

Method and other factors affecting 'good research' will arise indirectly as well as directly through funded projects. As we have explored already, many governments assess research in order to determine the amount of funding an institution may receive. For this reason, the definition of 'research' in the guidance notes for the 2021 Research Excellence Framework (REF) is one of the most relevant (Research Excellence Framework 2021), and it is important to notice a small but significant change from its earlier, 2001 version.

Note that the 2001 guidelines for the then named 'Research Assessment Exercise' defined research as:

> 'Research' for the purpose of the RAE is to be understood as original investigation undertaken in order to gain knowledge and understanding. It includes work of direct relevance to the needs of commerce and industry, as well as to the public and voluntary sectors; scholarship; the invention and generation of ideas, images, performances and artefacts including design, where these lead to new or substantially improved insights; and the use of existing knowledge in experimental development to produce new or substantially improved materials, devices, products and processes, including design and construction. It excludes routine testing and analysis of materials, components and processes, e.g., for the maintenance of national standards, as distinct from the development of new analytical techniques. It also excludes the development of teaching materials that do not embody original research.

At the time of writing, 2022, the REF updated definition is research is: 'For the purposes of the REF, research is defined as a process of investigation leading to new insights, *effectively shared*' [emphasis mine]. The definition goes on:

1. It includes work of direct relevance to the needs of commerce, industry, culture, society, and to the public and voluntary sectors; scholarship20; the invention and generation of ideas, images, performances, artefacts including design, where these lead to new or substantially improved insights; and the use of existing knowledge in experimental development to produce new or substantially improved materials, devices, products and processes, including design and construction. It excludes routine testing and routine analysis of materials, components and processes such as for the maintenance of national standards, as distinct from the development of new analytical techniques. It also excludes the development of teaching materials that do not embody original research.
2. It includes research that is published, disseminated or made publicly available in the form of assessable research outputs, and confidential reports (as defined in paragraph 261).

The small but critical difference is the addition of 'effectively shared' in its single-sentence definition, and the addition of point 3 in the longer definition, stressing dissemination. That difference is important when we realize that the governmental definition of research includes 'sharing'. As discussed in this book's opening chapter, the twin activities of publishing and funding are inseparable and together create successful career paths. That idea is reinforced here: to only conduct research is insufficient. The research data must be available to others, either through depositing data in recognized data banks or disseminating it through other means, such as publishing.

How research gets used

The usefulness of research and its relationship to 'good' depends on the role of the person and what he or she perceives that role to be. When teachers use research as examples for teaching, even 'bad' research can be 'good'.

Professional researchers based in institutions may 'use' research to increase their standing and therefore their likelihood of gaining funding. The student who wants to use the right research to please the right professor is doing much the same thing: both are seeking to increase a perception of their credibility and knowledge.

Good research thus satisfies the objectives of many different people and sectors. This does not in itself present an insurmountable problem where, say, the researcher is faced with conflicting objectives and definitions of what is good.

It was precisely that quality of multi-dimensional approaches to good research that was praised in a report on an ESRC-funded project led by Prof. Rod Rhodes in the Department of Politics at the University of Newcastle. Its objectives were to create a better understanding of both recent and long-term changes in the nature of the British government and how those compared with changes in similar governments in Europe. It also aimed to develop new theoretical perspectives and new research methods as well as encouraging interdisciplinary work and new researchers. A particular emphasis was placed on dissemination.

It is therefore apparent that what was 'good' about that research project would depend on a variety of aspects. An excerpt from the final evaluation provides an excellent example of how 'good' the project was in the view of its assessors:

> The Director's achievement in publishing alongside his grant-holder colleagues to the extent listed in the report is remarkable. Together with his

propagation of the Whitehall-programme within and beyond this country, it has provided much more than a mere complement to the projects' own achievements. Together, his work and theirs has constituted an academic campaign of real distinction, perhaps unique in British social science to date. Advances in methods, creating and lodging new data sets and achieving some training among the projects' junior researchers and associated PhD students are all covered in this report. The Council and the civil service have had an excellent return on their investment in the Whitehall-programme and its extension projects, both from the projects and the outstanding quality of the Programme's direction.

'Good' may be linked to subjective, qualitative statements which vary not only by person but by purpose. People evaluate and use research differently.

What are 'good' research methods?

Good research uses appropriate methods, and in its writing up the author makes the process transparent. Many examples of published research are not transparent. The choices you make about method will influence what you find, of course, but it will also influence the assessors' judgement about you. Are you competent enough to be able to evaluate a range of choices? Have you just grabbed what may be seen as a trendy approach without actually thinking about it? A funding proposal or journal paper needs to answer fundamental questions about 'method' before any judgement can be made. Why this approach? Why that sample? How do you intend to create that sample? What methods of enquiry will you use? Interviews? Surveys? And why are those methods appropriate? How will you evaluate them as the project unfolds, and will you be able to change them if they provide less effective than you had anticipated?

The main implication I would draw is that no method is value-free and therefore the scholar must not only become aware of his or her values but also make them transparent to, in this case, the assessor or editor. This brings a different meaning to the word 'good' and how we might define ethical research.

The area of ethics has been changing rapidly in recent years, and I look in more detail at some of the issues in the next chapter.

Good research data management and sharing

Another consideration relating to 'good' research is how the data you gather is managed in order to protect it and the rights of others and to enable sharing. Funders and publishers need to know how your data can be stored, shared, and the rights of others protected.

This is something that needs detailed thought and consultation with your own institution, and prospective applicants need to be prepared for the amount of time and thought it will take. Some funders provide questions to start you thinking, but in any case, the basic data management plan is likely to cover issues ranging from risk management, data storage mechanisms, compatibility with your intuition, involvement with relevant IT and library colleagues, data access, formatting, intellectual property issues, legal issues, evidence of conformance to relevant data protection regulations, at institutional, national and international levels, and so on. Similar questions are likely to arise when the paper is reviewed for publication.

Applicants and authors also need to think about how their data will be shared. Whether interview transcripts or survey results, funders expect that research paid for by public funds should be available to other researchers. This makes sense, particularly in fields where there may be overlap in research issues and sometimes a need to develop, chronologically, findings and theories.

In the UK, researchers funded by many of the Research Councils are contractually obligated to deposit their data in a central depository called ReShare, provided by the UK Data Service. This is an online data repository for archiving, publishing, and sharing research data. Part of the research proposal needs to specific how you have agreed with the UK Data Service what data you will be depositing and, if applicable, how confidentiality will be protected. You also need to review available data to ensure that the research you are proposing has not already been conducted, or that data available is insufficient for the question you are proposing. The research body, reasonably, wants to ensure it is not funding research that simply duplicates what is already available.

Researchers also need to demonstrate that they are observing their duties of care towards their research participants, particularly concerning confidentiality. This is usually more complicated than simply deleting someone's real name and inserting 'interviewee 1'. For research that proposes to illuminate real people's lives, for example, other descriptors such as age, gender, or social class may be necessary. Be prepared to consider those variations and explain to your funder or editor the method you used.

During recent years digital research conducted over the internet has created new forms of ethical concerns. Does watching someone's YouTube video constitute covert research? What about reading comments on people's blogs, or in response to Tweets or other posts? Once again, detailed guidance is given by institutions and funders, mostly relating to the degree with which the researcher influences online content without other people's knowledge or consent.

A recent example I was involved with involved Kim Harding, a sociology student whose doctoral studies I supervise at Goldsmiths, University of London. She decided to conduct her doctoral research on how vegans communicate their ethical beliefs digitally via YouTube. We noted that while 'The ethics of using publicly available content in internet research is a complicated and ever-changing landscape' (Harding and Day 2021, 3) the challenge needed to be met mainly because, as Patterson (2018, 765) suggested, the 'seemingly endless data points' of online spaces should not 'become disassociated from the individuals who breathe life into them'. Once again, as noted earlier, the key principles of being transparent and causing no harm were guiding principles. In this new and shifting territory, it is more important than ever to be clear in funding proposals and papers exactly how such ethical complexities will be navigated. In her case, Harding contacted a sample of YouTubers who met her criteria and agreed with those who responded that a transcript of their videos could be used.

Summary

I have discussed in this chapter that there is no single definition of good research. Good research is defined by those who assess it in particular situations and circumstances. When working to the needs of a funding body it is useful to find out as much as possible about the assessors.

However, 'good' is not purely situational. In looking at some of the terms used across various research councils and funding bodies, and the university research supervisors and professors I interviewed, some themes emerged.

The word 'interdisciplinary' (or cross-disciplinary, or multi-disciplinary) was used several times; the idea that research might be stronger if people brought skills and knowledge learned from one discipline to bear on an adjacent area. The notion of the research teams, and how they might, or have been, selected and managed, needs to be articulated.

Whether discussing large or small-scale research, empirical or ethnographic, detailed data analysis or, as Beverley Skeggs put it, 'just hanging around and talking … as much as possible', most people I spoke to use the term 'rigorous'. Whatever the approach, it must not be sloppy; it must be thoroughly thought through, without loose ends.

All funded research will have some kind of clear and visible output, and for that reason, another important term used is 'accessibility'. Outputs typically go beyond publication in a highly specialized learned journal. Research funding bodies need usually to demonstrate to their own funders, or trustees, that money has been well spent. This may well involve the sharing of some or all the written research output, and being able to say, clearly; this is what we did; this is how it will benefit people; this is how other researchers may use the data or take our findings further.

An important term also much used was 'transparency'. In other words, be clear about your limitations; be clear about your own interests and background. Don't bluff your readers. No research methods are value-free; the more transparent you are in discussing them, the closer to 'good' your research is likely to be. Pay attention to research ethics, both in the detail of your research design and dissemination, and also in the deeper, wider concerns of diversity and inclusivity.

Finally, when I conducted workshops about research funding and publications, I have been surprised that participants often know little about the criteria funding bodies or journal reviewers use for rating research. The implication is that a lot of time and money is being wasted, and important work is not being funded or published. In the next chapters, we will look at how to better target potential funders and journals and articulate the proposed match to make it apparent that a funding or publishing relationship will benefit all parties.

Action points

1. Consider how you, your institution, and any funders you know define 'excellence'.
2. Check at least three journal websites for any definitions relating to 'good research' or 'research excellence'.
3. Consider how your research methods could be considered to be 'good'.

References

Cornwall, Marie (2010). 'From the editor: Ten most likely ways an article submission fails to live up to publishing standard', *Journal for the Scientific Study of Religion*, 49(4): i–v.

Ferretti, Federico, Ângela Guimarães Pereira, Dániel Vértesy and Sjoerd Hardeman (2018 October). 'Research excellence indicators: time to reimagine the "making of"?', *Science and Public Policy*, 45(5): 731–741. https://doi.org/10.1093/scipol/scy007

Harding, Kim, and Abby Day. (2021). 'Vegan YouTubers performing ethical beliefs', *Religions*, 12: 7. https://dx.doi.org/ 10.3390/rel12010007

Patterson, Ashley N. (2018). 'YouTube generated video clips as qualitative research data: One researcher's reflections on the process'. *Qualitative Inquiry* 24: 759–67.

Research Excellence Framework (2021). 'Index of revisions to the "Guidance on submissions" (2019/01)'. Available at: https://www.ref.ac.uk/media/1447/ref-2019_01-guidance-on-submissions.pdf

Tuhiwai Smith, Linda (2012). *Decolonizing Methodologies: Research and Indigenous Peoples*. London: Zed Books.

UK Research and Innovation (2021) 'Survey findings of the impact of COVID-19 on researchers'. Available at: https://www.ukri.org/news/survey-findings-of-the-impact-of-covid-19-on-researchers/

UK Research and Innovation (2022) 'Guidance for applicants, students and award-holders impacted by the pandemic'. Available at: https://www.ukri.org/news-and-events/tackling-the-impact-of-covid-19/guidance-for-applicants-and-awardholders-impacted-by-the-pandemic/

5 DIVERSITY AND INCLUSION IN RESEARCH

Introduction

Conducting ethical research

Check the ethics statements of your proposed funder requests. These may differ between funders, and also depending on whether your research involves human participants. While most funders will assume full ethics approval will be sought and obtained from relevant institutions after the proposal is approved, they will still want to see detail on the application form. For example, the ESRC in the UK has guidance notes on its website publicly available even before you need to begin the application process (Joint Electronic Submissions 2022):

> ESRC expects that full consideration is given to any ethical matters in the research it funds and that, where appropriate, the research meets key ethical principles and is approved by ethical authorities. Applicants are asked to confirm that consideration has been given to ethical issues and to explain any issues raised, together with the form of ethical approval that has already been obtained or would be sought if the proposal were to be funded. If ethics approval is regarded as unnecessary, justification should be expressed with reference to the exemptions set out in ESRC's Research Ethics Framework document (https://www.ukri.org/councils/esrc/guidance-for-applicants/research-ethics-guidance/), which contains a full explanation of ESRC's approach and guidance for applicants. Referees will be asked to give special attention to this statement about ethical issues.

Those undertaking medical research will need to follow guidelines specified by the funder, such as the Medical Research Council, and individual regulatory bodies.

A guiding principle for most research is that human participants are aware that they are being researched and that no harm will be done. For example,

DOI: 10.4324/9781003259718-6

such principles lead the American Anthropological Association's ethics statement on its website: (American Anthropological Association n.d.):

> AAA is committed to helping all anthropologists have access to quality information regarding methodological and ethical best practices. The Association's Principles of Professional Responsibility include:
> Do No Harm
> Be Open and Honest Regarding Your Work
> Obtain Informed Consent and Necessary Permissions
> Weigh Competing Ethical Obligations Due Collaborators and Affected Parties
> Make Your Results Accessible
> Protect and Preserve Your Records
> Maintain Respectful and Ethical Professional Relationships
> Each of these principles is more fully defined in the full AAA Statement on Ethics (2012). The Association has also established a Policy on Sexual Harassment and Sexual Assault.

Long gone are the days when participants were tricked into participating in research without their knowledge and consent, sometimes with disastrous consequences. Those studies have been well-publicized and rightly criticized, but what is less discussed is the impact on the researchers themselves. Anyone observing people in a public place may do so without obtaining the consent of the observed. We all do that every day. But the lines are not always clear when it comes to using those observations in academic research. For anyone employing research assistants, there are important ethical concerns. As Nicole Podschuweit (2021, 309) notes:

> Two aspects that are neglected in the ethical debates about the dangers of old and new forms of covert observation are, however, the perspective of the research subjects and – especially with regard to studies involving human observers – the special responsibility of the investigator towards his or her research assistants, who in most cases are students.

Such attention to those debates, and a discussion about how to mitigate the stress that research assistants may suffer, would fit well within a research proposal and in a published paper. It is an example of how applicants, and authors, can be seen to be attentive and professional in their approaches.

Even not so obvious forms of possibly covert research need to be considered and anticipated in the proposal process. How, for example, will an anthropologist or sociologist account for 'informed consent' when a private gathering suddenly becomes larger, and many who were not part of the original research project are present? How are they to consider issues of dynamic, evolving consent? Those are questions to discuss with project partners and, if relevant, one's supervisor. They are questions assessors may consider and therefore need to be anticipated and written into the application.

Some forms of research can potentially harm researchers as well as those they research. The British Sociological Association is clear in their advice that such risks need to be considered:

> Social researchers face a range of potential risks to their safety. Safety issues need to be considered in the design and conduct of social research projects and procedures should be adopted to reduce the risk to researchers, including, importantly, any research assistants employed.
> (British Sociological Association 2017)

Specific reference to an institution's and professional bodies' ethics statements are useful additions. These demonstrate that the applicant is aware of wider ethical issues, and where to find information about them. Many of those professional bodies share similar general principles and some point to each other to reinforce the importance of wider, international norms. For example, the British Sociological Association explicitly references in its Ethics statement the Academy of Social Sciences, the Social Research Association, the American Sociological Association, the Association of Social Anthropologists of the UK and the Commonwealth, and the British Psychological Society.

Ethical consideration must also be given to research matters beyond the process of data gathering and, increasingly, funders and journals expect applicants and authors to be clear about how they manage such issues.

Demonstrating ethical inclusivity

One criticism I often make when reviewing a funding proposal or a journal paper is the extent to which the author intends to incorporate other voices, in field research or in theoretical reviews. How aware are applicants or authors of the now significant move to ensure any research is ethical because it recognizes, and to some extent ameliorates the often-privileged position of the researcher?

Approaches within feminist epistemology, for example, have long called attention to how knowledge is produced, not 'found' as if it is already complete, waiting to be discovered (Ackerly and True 2010). A feminist epistemological approach may also overtly embrace values such as subjectivity and normativity. A normative stance acknowledges the intertwined, subjective nature of research and will take up a position: some kinds of research methods may be simply wrong, they suggest. A now classic example was critique mounted against the conventional practice of interviewing. When Ann Oakley (1981) explored the practice in her research with pregnant women, she discovered what she argued was a contradiction in terms. Oakley was concerned with the ethics and power relationships of interviewing, noting that what is good for the interviewer is not necessarily good for the person being interviewed. The research method of interviewing stems from a masculinist viewpoint that privileges such notions of objectivity and distance she argued. Further, she observed that the process is rarely transparent: 'Very few sociologists who employ interview data actually bother to describe in detail the process of interviewing itself' (Oakley 1981, 31 and see also, for her reflections on this many years later, Oakley 2016).

Another person who drew attention to the importance of subjectivity was William Foote Whyte whose *Street Corner Society* (1943) has influenced scholarship and policy since its publication in 1943. The result of four years of participant observation in the area he described as 'Cornerville', Boston, Whyte's aim was to map out the social structure of the community, at a time when many such inner urban areas were dismissed as 'slums' and thought to be a 'formidable mass of confusion' (Whyte 1993, xvi). Using ethnographic methods, Whyte lived in the neighbourhood and by observing and participating in daily activities he found that the area was a 'highly organised and integrated social system' (Whyte 1993, xvi). As Whyte became assimilated into the society, learning the local Italian language and participating in activities, he began to lose some of his 'outsider' status. He writes: 'I began as a non-participating observer. As I became accepted into the community, I found myself becoming almost a non-observing participant' (Whyte 1993, 321). This relates to more than simply learning the language. Another implication concerns the mask we choose to wear. If we are to learn more about implicit beliefs, about meaning in different cultures and local knowledge, then we need to have more than 'right' methods to do it; we need humility. This may be determined less by our theoretical knowledge as sociologists and more by how we listen and generate discussion. It is how British sociologist Beverley Skeggs began her research with working class women:

> I knew little about methodology and began the research by just hanging around and talking to the women as much as possible.
>
> (Skeggs, 1997, 22)

That style of inductive research gets right to the heart of how we see our roles as researchers, funders, teachers, and students. It also highlights the importance of opening up research methods to co-participants. It is a commonplace to assert that methods or findings are open to the scrutiny of research participants and affected other parties. But how exactly will this happen? How much time and money will be invested in those processes?

Such conversations and practices continue to affect what is being defined as 'good' research.

Ethics of diversity, equality, and decolonization

Recent campaigns to 'liberate', 'diversify', or 'decolonize' the curriculum have drawn attention to a troubled anthropological (and, to a lesser extent, sociological) colonial history. As Talal Asad noted (1973, 11), 'There was a time when social anthropology could, and did, define itself unambiguously as the study of primitive societies.' As Asad (1973, 16) continues his critique, he notes that anthropologists had situated their own history in Enlightenment ideals, ignoring its unequal power encounter between 'the West and the Third World which goes back to the emergence of bourgeois Europe, an encounter in which colonialism is only one historical moment' and where the anthropologist did not interrogate the colonial system itself. Another early contributor to that conversation was Diane Lewis (1993, 581) who argued that anthropologists were failing to notice and respond to their past, even while others were:

> Disillusionment with the discipline from outside is paralleled by growing criticism from within. Most of this criticism, appearing increasingly in the United States since the second half of the 1960s, has focused on the failure of anthropologists to come to terms with and accept responsibility for the political implications of their work.

Some of those implications are material as well as intellectual. The process of 'colonization' includes both material and epistemic means to suppress and reinforce 'otherness' (Said 1978). Lewis drew attention to the commonly accepted, and for many, the only valid form of anthropological practice: the conduct of fieldwork in faraway places. She described this process as ethically dubious, consisting as it does of researchers visiting distant places, thanks to tax-free research grants, and studying indigenous people as 'others'. Those 'others', however, typically do not benefit from the research conducted by the scholar whose position and remuneration are enriched as a result.

Another imbalance is caused by, in this case, a Eurocentric, Global North neglect of the original contributions to theory and practice that can be made by academics in the Global South. Raewyn Connell (2007) picked up this theme particularly arguing that the intellectual frameworks used in 'northern' sociology are presented as universal and ignore different frameworks developed in 'southern' sociology. They suggest that Eurocentric scholars need to go beyond 'the tendency to keep a northern conceptual framework while putting in more southern content' (Connell, 2018, 404).

Sociologist Rima Saini has explored complex identities, particularly those of British South Asians (Saini 2022). I was particularly struck with how, at a symposium we both attended, she succinctly summarized for the teachers present the key concepts of 'colonization' as:

> the act of taking control of an area or a country that is not your own, especially using force, and sending people from your own country to live there. This also involves imposing values, views and practices on the indigenous population.

To 'decolonize', she explained, was to reverse that process and for education, this meant 'the process of reversing colonization in teaching, learning and curricula'. Importantly, the act of decolonizing research methods meant 'removing colonial assumptions about what is important and what counts as 'valid' data'. She elaborated:

> Decolonisation in education also means thinking about the ways we gather knowledge – in other words, how our approaches to research are rooted in the preferences and priorities of researchers and scholars with power and resources. This feeds into the knowledge that forms the basis of our formal sociological education.

Why are some methods, such as statistical analysis, regarded as better, more 'factual' and more reliable, she asks, than other forms of data, such as ethnographic, visual or interview? She challenges the idea that quantitative, survey-based research is 'objective':

> In surveys, for example, how and why do we tend to frame identities like race (Black/White) and gender (Female/Male) in simplistic ways? How does this form our understanding of social inequalities in helpful and unhelpful ways?

Such questions, and such work, demand a deep restructuring of how knowledge is created. Gurminda Bhambra called for moves to '(re)structure global narratives' that currently dominate discourse to include 'the empirical connections forged through histories of colonialism, enslavement, dispossession and appropriation' (Bhambra, 2014, 149).

Scholars generally accept those criticisms as valid, but there has been a dearth of publications focusing on practical steps scholars and institutions can take. In my book edited with Lois Lee, Dave Thomas, and Jim Spickard (2022), we argued that universities and individual researchers need to address the deeply embedded problems which affect the extent to which people are admitted to the circles of academia – including teaching, research, and publishing. While such discriminatory practices are often not visible, they are nonetheless effective at keeping White male, Global North dominance. Euro-American universities privilege Euro-American knowledge and norms, with curricula and publications relying mainly on the work of northern scholars. In so doing, universities also obscure the specific power relations that created Euro-American geo-political dominance in the first place: histories of exploitation, theft, and slavery. They are thus often mistaking hegemony, for 'quality'. The standards they set, both for scholarship and publishing, present Euro-American criteria as 'world-leading' rather than particular and parochial.

Although much has been said and written about diversifying or decolonizing the academy, progress has been slow and limited. In 2020 it was reported that only one-fifth of British universities said that they were taking part in such initiatives, and amongst those who were, their actions were limited. Nevertheless, worldwide the movement gained pace in 2020 when millions of people around the world marched as part of Black Lives Matter (2022) to protest against police brutality and wider forms of current and historical oppression.

The edited collection mentioned above (Day et al. 2022) contained chapters written by people who have worked to diversify their own, and their institutions, teaching, writing, and research practices. These included initiatives to expand publishing criteria and incorporate a more diverse range of voices. For example, to guide people in diversifying their curricula, Karen Schucan Bird (2022) asked academics to consider how diverse is their reading lists. She suggests that the practice of interrogating reading lists is a useful initial step towards diversifying or decolonizing curricula. Through a project undertaken at her own university, she and her team examined the gender, ethnicity, and geographical location of all authors included on a reading list for a post-graduate module on social science research methods.

The team analyzed the characteristics of each author cited. While they used for their criteria salient characteristics found on other reviews of reading lists, such as gender, geographical location, and ethnicity, they noted that there remains a range of other categories that could be interrogated. These included nine characteristics that warrant protection from discrimination and harassment in higher education as part of the Equality Act 2010 in England and Wales: age, disability, gender reassignment, pregnancy and maternity, race, religion or belief, sex, sexual orientation, marriage or civil partnership. The authors noted that other researchers are arguing for such coverage, of at least disability and sexuality, and for the extension of the number of characteristics to include social class.

To help students and early career scholars review their own research practices, Sara Ewing at Goldsmiths, University of London, runs courses for students she calls 'Decolonizing Research Methods'. She discusses (2022, 128) how she took two main themes in most students' social science research – the 'Enlightenment' and related historical processes – and showed how 'a decolonial critique of Enlightenment and historical foundations asserts that, rather than these ideas simply being disseminated, they must be questioned and reinterpreted in context'. Because she writes (2022, 129): 'Traditional research methods privilege discrete and transferrable measures that rely on prior research, conceptual precedent, and perceived disciplinary value', students are taught to question that research, precedents, and values:

> The production and exchange of knowledge can thus be considered a means to acknowledge and validate the liminal space in which ideas and identities are formed. This approach delinks the construction of knowledge from the colonial matrix of classification and domination. As such, a decolonizing response to a Eurocentric research paradigm requires the careful deconstruction of the social and conceptual hierarchies that underpin Western epistemology.

Gurminder Bhambra (2014) posed such questions when she challenged the fiction and idealization of individually created knowledges about modernity and rationalization, themselves consequences of colonization (and see here Quijano 2007).

Many academics draw on the foundational work of scholars such as Walter Mignolo (2011) who have argued that apparently neutral empirical and historical data is often presented as if they are products of a natural, inevitable evolution of humanity, rather than the weapons they have been and continue to be used to inform and justify colonial missions.

A radical conceptual shift in a university's approach to diversity, inclusion, and decolonization is required to change the idea of the singular 'uni' versity to one of a 'pluri' versity, Achille Mbembe (2016, 36–37) suggested:

> a process of knowledge production that is open to epistemic diversity. It … does not necessarily abandon the notion of universal knowledge for humanity, but … embraces it via a horizontal strategy of openness to dialogue among different epistemic traditions. To decolonize the university is therefore to reform it with the aim of creating a less provincial and more open critical cosmopolitan pluriversalism – a task that involves the radical refounding of our ways of thinking and a transcendence of our disciplinary divisions.

This requires more effort and change than updating reading lists or engaging with more people of colour, Heidi Mirza argues. She says that while higher education is still constituted by spaces in which women, indigenous scholars and people of colour (POC) are treated as strangers or intruders, other, subversive, strategies may occur:

Heidi Mirza (2015, 8) says that in higher education contexts where women, black students, POC, and indigenous scholars are treated as strangers, or intruders, transformative strategies will inevitably emerge.

> In their space on the margin, with their quiet and subversive acts of care and 'other ways of knowing,' these women [and black students, POC, and indigenous scholars] operate within, between, under, and alongside the mainstream educational and labor market structures, subverting, renaming and reclaiming opportunities … through the transformative pedagogy of 'raising the race'.

Academics may decide in their own ways how to respond to those ideas, but it is clear that, increasingly, academics worldwide are seeking such changes. The move is being felt globally across disciplines as Ryuko Kubota (2020, 718) notes, from 'music, art, history, science, research theories, and methodologies' with serious, negative consequences. She (Kubota 2020, 716) explains that:

> Individual discrimination in an institution both reflects and produces deeper systemic inequalities; at the same time, epistemological racism in our system of knowledge production and circulation excludes not only racialized but also white scholars institutionally and individually in their scholarly engagement outside of white Eurocentric norms.

Jim Spickard (2002, 163–164) suggests that anthropologists have gone further than sociologists to undo the harm of their colonial past and create, through earnest engagements in dialogue, more collaborative, ethical works:

> Post-colonial particularizing anthropology has embraced equality, while much particularizing sociology has not. Anthropological ethnographers once wrote as if they served the Empire, but many do so no longer. Sociological ethnographers, for the most part, still participate in a discourse that honors the middle class.

He warns that a generalizing social science 'produces a clash of worldviews that implicitly belittles religious understandings. And because it does not recognize these understandings' epistemological equality, it furthers the colonial project'.

How individual scholars and institutions respond is taking many forms, although work on practical steps is generally sparse (but see the edited volume by Day et al. 2022 for recent examples). Sarah Ahmed, for example, concluded that because scholarship has been unfairly dominated by white men, scholars should work harder to avoid reproducing whiteness in academic research. She adopts a strict citation policy, saying 'I do not cite any white men. … In this book, I cite feminists of color' (Ahmed, 2017, 15). Recognizing that not all scholars, particularly early career researchers, may feel able to take such a radical approach, Januschka Schmidt (2022, 176) suggests adopting a more 'moderate' approach, whereby a 'critical citation practice' asking:

> that we are conscious of whom we cite and actively challenge the way we cite throughout the research process in a structural manner. I suggest that researchers approach a literature review and their citations in a three- step, sequential fashion: 1. focus on authors from the community one investigates (this step is less relevant for research in the natural sciences and formal sciences); 2. consult literature by disadvantaged groups; and only then 3. consider the advantaged and established canon.

The dominance of journals from the Global North in libraries and their accompanying index tools skew the perception of where and how knowledge is created. Paige Mann (2022, 186–202) provides a detailed analysis of the problem, beginning with citation indexes which contain only a small selection of all publications worldwide, and yet their 'impact factors' influence both the buying behaviour of libraries and prominence in databases. This, in turn, affects people's careers and the reproduction of certain authorial and related theoretical voices. A. Suresh Canagarajah (2002, 12–13) describes this problem from a personal perspective:

> I began to experience the inequalities in publishing most intensely when I returned to Sri Lanka from postgraduate work in the United States. Though I faced a lot of difficulties in conducting research and writing, these matters could not be addressed in the articles I wrote [for Northern audiences]. In a few instances, in order to explain the discursive differences in my work, I mentioned in a paragraph or two the problems of periphery scholars in conducting research and publishing according to center requirements. But eventually, I had to omit these statements in the final drafts as reviewers felt that they were irrelevant to the focus of my paper … [S]uch publishing assumptions and practices place hurdles in the way of addressing the concerns relating to different contexts of knowledge production.

Authors seeking to change that dominance can, for example, spend more time and care on their bibliographic sources, working to find those voices that tend to be muted by the noisy dominance of Euro-American journals. The publisher of this book, Taylor & Francis, encouraged such practices. In its notes of guidance for authors, they say:

> We believe in social justice, diversity, equity, and inclusion, and we support ethically responsible research. Many referencing guides include advice for using bias-free language, and we would encourage authors to consider this in their work [...] We also encourage authors to consider diversity in their selection of contributors, texts, references, images, and case study examples. Any language or imagery which could be considered bigoted, or prejudiced, including racist or sexist language and imagery, may be challenged, and flagged for removal. We do of course recognise that some work will by necessity engage with or quote such material for the purposes of critical analysis

The decolonizing movement has rightly been gaining pace. The institutions of the Global North and West remain dominated by a small elite, with a much narrower set of perspectives and interests than are found in diverse populations. From a publishing perspective, the problem extends beyond citation practices. Scholars need access to journals and books, but because of the high prices demanded by publishers, increasingly fewer universities can afford to give their students and staff the full access they need (see, for more detail, Mann 2022).

Campaigners have, rightly, argued that research should be available through Open Access, but in practice, this has created more barriers. The current approach is to levy a fee on authors for submitting papers. The fee is often built into funded research budgets, and therefore the funder (typically a government research council) pays the fee. Or, in the case of unfunded research, the submission or publication fee merely transfers the cost from readers to authors. Non-elite authors lack institutional support to pay those fees, and therefore their research becomes locked out.

A second barrier is more insidious. It results from the current hegemony of English as the international language of scholarship and from the publishers' policy of soliciting most academic reviewers and copyeditors from the Global North. These reviewers and editors ensure that prospective authors not only cite the 'correct' people in their papers but follow rigid house-style rules and often unfamiliar (to those outside the elite) spelling and grammatical conventions.

Serial commas? Upper or lower case following a colon? En or em dashes? Semi-colons or dashes? These often-arcane devices, drilled into people attending schools that reinforce both grammar and its cultural capital, do not interfere with understanding, and yet are often imposed by publishers, further raising the barriers.

These obstacles combine with a range of so-called 'disciplinary standards' that privilege the work of those most frequently published and cited, who, again, tend to be the Northern, predominantly White male scholarly elite. This is particularly true when a discipline's language, or jargon, is excessively opaque (Kornei 2021).

Frantz Fanon (2008, 9) called attention to the positionality of colonized people whose acceptance by the colonizers depends on the extent of their willingness to subvert their indigenous identities:

> Every colonized people – in other words, every people in whose soul an inferiority complex has been created by the death and burial of its local cultural originality – finds itself face to face with the language of the civilizing nation; that is, with the culture of the mother country. The colonized is elevated above his jungle status in proportion to his adoption of the mother country's cultural standards.

This situation is likely to worsen as a result of the COVID-19 global pandemic. While this damaged economies worldwide, it will likely reduce money and opportunities for research and training for all but those from elite Global North schools.

That is one reason that I encourage scholars and institutions to open more spaces – on editorial boards, review panels, and departmental and institutional committees – to diverse scholars. I return to this again in Chapter 12.

Summary

This chapter has discussed notions of ethics in research, from several viewpoints. Some ethical standards appear unproblematic and are defined by institutions and organizations, mainly to protect research participants and researchers from harm. Other considerations of 'ethics' explore more deeply embedded problems relating to unequal power relations between, mainly, the Global North/West and the Global South. How scholars and institutions respond to such inequalities may vary, but the recent calls to 'diversify' and 'decolonize' the curriculum are gaining momentum worldwide. Some practical steps, such as actively reviewing which voices and theories dominate research, teaching, and publications are recommended. Structural, systemic change, however, will occur only when power structures of the institutions are disrupted to include more diverse participation.

Action points

1. Review your own emerging publications and research to identify whose voices dominate.
2. Address the conceptual and theoretical work certain voices create and consider the extent to which these remain embedded in elite institutions and histories of the Global North.

References

Ackerly, Brooke and Jacqui True (2010). *Doing Feminist Research in Political and Social Science*. New York. Palgrave Macmillan.

Ahmed, Sara (2017). *Living a Feminist Life*. Durham, NC and London: Duke University Press.

American Anthropological Association (n.d.). Anthropological ethics – Learn and teach. Available at: https://www.americananthro.org/ethics-and-methods#:~:text=Do%20No%20Harm,Due%20Collaborators%20and%20Affected%20Parties [accessed 22 April 2022].

Asad, Talal, ed. (1973). *Anthropology and the Colonial Encounter*. Atlantic Highlands, NJ: Ithaca Press and Humanities Press.

Bhambra, Gurminder (2014). *Connected Sociologies*. London: Bloomsbury.

Bird, Karen Schucan (2022). 'How "diverse" is your reading list? Tools, tips, and challenges'. In *Diversity, Inclusion, and Decolonisation: Practical Tools for Improving*

Teaching, Research and Scholarship, eds. Abby Day, Lois Lee, David Thomas and James Spickard. Bristol: Bristol University Press, pp. 139–158.

Black Lives Matter (2022). Available at: https://blacklivesmatter.com/

British Sociological Association (2017). BSA statement of ethical practice. Available at: https://www.britsoc.co.uk/media/24310/bsa_statement_of_ethical_practice.pdf [accessed 22 February 2022].

Canagarajah, A. Suresh (2002). *A Geopolitics of Academic Writing*. Pittsburgh: University of Pittsburgh Press.

Connell, Raewyn (2007). *Southern Theory: The Global Dynamics of Knowledge in Social Science*. Cambridge: Polity.

Connell, Raewyn (2018). 'Decolonizing sociology', *Contemporary Sociology*, 47(4): 399–407.

Day, Abby, Lois Lee, David Thomas and James Spickard, eds. (2022). *Diversity, Inclusion, and Decolonisation: Practical Tools for Improving Teaching, Research and Scholarship*. Bristol: Bristol University Press.

Ewing, Sara (2022). 'Decolonizing research methods: Practices, challenges, and opportunities'. In *Diversity, Inclusion, and Decolonisation: Practical Tools for Improving Teaching, Research and Scholarship*, eds. Day, Abby, Lois Lee, David Thomas and James Spickard. Bristol: Bristol University Press, pp. 181–202.

Fanon, Frantz (2008). *Black Skin, White Masks* (10th edn). London: Pluto Press.

Joint Electronic Submissions (2022). *Ethical Information*. Available at: https://je-s.rcuk.ac.uk/handbook/pages/GuidanceonCompletingaStandardG/EthicalInformation.htm

Kornei, Katherine (2021). 'Are you confused by scientific jargon? So are scientists', *New York Times*, 13 April, p. D2. [online] Available at: https://nyti.ms/2PnI pFV [accessed 26 April 2021].

Kubota, Ryuko (2020). 'Confronting epistemological racism, decolonizing scholarly knowledge: Race and gender in applied linguistics', *Applied Linguistics*, 41(5): 712–732.

Lewis, Diane (1973). 'Anthropology and colonialism', *Current Anthropology*, 14(5): 581–602.

Mann, P. (2022). 'Scholarship in a globalized world: The publishing ecosystem and alternatives to the oligopoly'. In *Diversity, Inclusion, and Decolonisation: Practical Tools for Improving Teaching, Research and Scholarship*, eds. Abby Day, Lois Lee, David Thomas and James Spickard. Bristol: Bristol University Press, pp. 267–292.

Mbembe, Achele (2016). 'Decolonizing the university: New directions', *Arts and Humanities in Higher Education*, 15(1): 29–41.

Mignolo, Walter D. (2011). *The Darker Side of Western Modernity: Global Futures, Decolonial Options*. Durham, NC: Duke University Press.

Mirza, Heidi S. (2015). 'Decolonizing higher education: Black feminism and the intersectionality of race and gender', *Journal of Feminist Scholarship*, 7/8: 1–12.

Oakley, Ann (1981). 'Interviewing women: A contradiction in terms'. In *Doing Feminist Research*, ed. Helen Roberts. London: Routledge & Kegan Paul, pp. 30–61.

Oakley, Ann (2016). 'Interviewing women again: Power, time and the gift', *Sociology*, 50: 195–213.

Podschuweit, Nicole (2021). 'How ethical challenges of covert observations can be met in practice', *Research Ethics*, 17(3): 309–327.

Quijano, Aníbal (2007). 'Coloniality and modernity/rationality', *Cultural Studies*, 21(2): 168–178.

Said, Edward W. (1978). *Orientalism: Western Conceptions of the Occident*. New York: Pantheon.

Saini, Rima (2022). 'The racialisation of class and the racialisation of the nation: Ethnic minority identity formation across the British South Asian middle classes', *South Asian Diaspora*, 14(2): 245–266.

Schmidt, Januschka (2022). 'Whom we cite: A reflection on the limits and potentials of critical citation practices'. In *Diversity, Inclusion, and Decolonisation: Practical Tools for Improving Teaching, Research and Scholarship*, eds. Abby Day, Lois Lee, David Thomas and James Spickard. Bristol: Bristol University Press, pp. 109–124.

Skeggs, Beverley (1997). *Formations of Class and Gender: Becoming Respectable*. London: Sage.

Spickard, James V. (2002). 'Human rights through a religious lens: A programmatic argument', *Social Compass,* 49(2): 227–238.

Whyte, William Foote (1943). *Street Corner Society: The Social Structure of an Italian Slum*. Chicago, IL: University of Chicago Press.

6   A SENSE OF PURPOSE

Introduction

Most papers submitted to an academic journal are rejected. Most funding proposals are also rejected. Fortunately, we know why that is so and how we can minimize our risks of ending up in the bin. There is an old adage that says if we do not know where we are going, any road will do. But if we have our destination firmly in mind, we can use maps to help us navigate.

This chapter explores several key success factors in writing research papers and proposals. The 'proposal-writing' stage, particularly in a funding context, comes late in the process. By the time you sit down to write a proposal, you should be clear about who your funder is, what is required and how you need to position your work.

Ask professional writers to sit down and write a few thousand words and they will start asking questions. A few thousand words about what? A few thousand words for whom? A few thousand words to achieve which objective? Yet, many novice writers complain that they cannot sit down to write a few thousand words because they are suffering from 'writer's block'. The expression is a strange one that means little to professional writers. Were they to wait for some mystical muse to sprinkle a little fairy dust on their computer they would still be waiting, but they are not. They are the ones with their pieces finished and published while everyone else is waiting for their mysterious writer's block to melt away.

Unfortunately, writing seems mysterious to those who do not do it regularly. It seems that people who do not write regularly can conclude that they are not writers. How often have you heard someone say, or said yourself, 'I am not a writer', as if a writer is a completely separate breed. For those who do write, especially for those who earn their living at it, it is a job like any other. Sometimes their writing would not escape the critical scrutiny of the average English Literature undergraduate. Take a closer look at how best-selling novelists write. The quality of the prose can be mediocre, even poor at times, but the story itself, the pace and the well-developed

DOI: 10.4324/9781003259718-7

characterizations captivate millions of readers. These are writers who know what they are going to say, and work hard at it, every day. As Thomas Edison once said, genius is 1 per cent inspiration and 99 per cent perspiration.

Experienced writers do not have 'blocks'. They may have lost the thread of what they are trying to say, they may realize that they need more information about a certain point which they will fill in later, but they are not blocked by an extraordinary force beyond their control. People who have writer's block are really being blocked by a lack of understanding about what needs to be said. They have lost their focus. They may have 'thinker's block' or 'focus block'.

Back to basics

It is surprising, considering that we have all at some stage gone through primary school, that so much can be forgotten about our first lessons in communication. It seems that once we enter university, we somehow think we can no longer follow the simple rules we learned at school. Indeed, for some people, the very idea that communication should follow simple rules seems to contradict the ethos of higher education. Suddenly, our language becomes more convoluted and dreary, we find ourselves reaching for the thesaurus to find a longer word which will replace the shorter, more familiar word and, worst of all, our writing seems to turn into a game we are playing with the reader: if we really waffle on for five thousand words using the most syllables per sentence we can find, and if we ramble our way through the paper with no obvious sense of direction, will we trick our readers into thinking that we are more clever than they are?

No. Our readers, if we should be so unlucky to escape the remonstrations of editors and reviewers first, and therefore benefit from their free professional advice, will simply become frustrated and bored. They will never discover the essential quality of the research or the benefits it may confer on them. They will give up or, if they are forced to read it through a tutor's direction or the demands of their own research, they will not like it much.

This chapter and the next deal with the two criteria of quality that span all disciplines, all forms of papers, and all funding proposals. These chapters represent the most compelling implication of my formal and informal research into academic publishing and funding. What I have discovered was simple, but sometimes not easy to apply. All other qualities being met, the most important concerns of reviewers are:

- What is this paper/proposal about?
- Why does it matter?

For example, the Gödel Prize is awarded annually for outstanding journal articles in the area of theoretical computer science. In 2005, it was awarded to Noga Alon, Yossi Matias, and Mario Szegedy for their paper: 'The space complexity of approximating the frequency moments' (Alon et al. 1999). The judges' comments referred to the simplicity, elegance, and wide applicability of its techniques which set a standard for future work in the field.

The lead author, Prof. Noga Alon is now at Princeton University. He is a member of the Editorial Boards of more than a dozen journals, has published hundreds of research papers, and has won prestigious international awards for his work. When I asked him what advice he would give to prospective authors, he said it was to see publishing as a natural outcome of good work 'which in my area (Mathematics and Computer Science) means to prove interesting results, suggest intriguing open problems and try to solve existing ones, and develop useful techniques and algorithms'.

Imagine how much good work might be rejected simply because the author does not address those important points: interesting, intriguing, useful. This may remind us of one of the definitions of 'good research' I discussed in Chapter 4. A good research paper or proposal is engaging. Its purpose and importance are immediately obvious to the reader. Editors and funding assessors will likely reject papers or proposals simply because the author or authors did not explain why they were writing the paper and what it all means. Sometimes, that is because they have not considered for themselves the purpose of the paper or proposal, other than perhaps to meet a demand to publish or to bring in research money. They have not moved beyond the level of immediate need. They may have determined that publishing or funding is important, and they have motivated themselves sufficiently to write something, but they have not considered the purpose of the paper or its implications from the readers' perspectives. Ultimately, they have failed to communicate.

As the pressure to publish and be funded increases and the flow of papers and proposals expands, reviewers may have less time to spend reading papers and proposals. Faced with several alternatives to achieve the same goal – that is, several papers or proposals on the same subject from the same sort of people – the reviewer will naturally prefer the ones that are most readable. If it is not immediately apparent what the paper or proposal is about, who can blame the weary reviewer who puts it aside, only to find that the next paper or proposal they read is clear, engaging and ethical? The earlier one that was too vague or incoherent will likely not get a second chance.

Many journal sites are clear about the importance of setting out the purpose at the outset. The *South African Journal of Economic and Management Sciences* (*SAJEMS*), Submission Guidelines (n.d.) for example, advises authors to ensure that the paper's Introduction 'should put the focus of the manuscript into a broader context and explain its social and scientific value'. In this case, the journal advice combined both significant criteria for journal excellence: purpose and implications.

The following examples are direct quotations from reviewers' reports, several of hundreds I collected during research for this book and at workshops worldwide and illustrate the reaction from reviewers when others do not follow such advice:

- 'Lacks a sense of purpose'
- 'Authors do not explain why they are writing this paper'
- 'Not clear where this is going or why'

Clearly, we want to avoid receiving those kinds of comments. Let's see how.

Reflecting on her long tenure as editor of the *Journal for the Scientific Study of Religion*, Marie Cornwall (2010) offers aspiring authors advice on getting published.

The biggest question reviewers and readers will have is what the paper is about, and why it is important. Cornwall describes this as the 'take-away'. I suggest here that much of her advice applies equally to funding proposals. Authors, and applicants, need to ask themselves why their paper should be published, or their proposal funded. How does the paper, or proposed project, contribute to the accumulation of knowledge? Why, Cornwall asks, should the reader keep reading? She suggests authors get to the point soon, at least within the first four pages, with a statement such as: 'This research contributes to the literature on… by…'.

Cornwall describes the paper as being similar to a good short story or novel, where the reader soon develops a sense of what may be coming because the author has provided some 'foreshadowing'. A direct 'take-away' statement, she says, helps the paper's (or proposal's) chances of being easily assessed by a reviewer who needs to judge the extent to which the author has accomplished what they set out to achieve. Cornwall says she can judge the clarity of the author's 'take-away' by the ways reviewers respond to it. A good indicator of how well the 'take-away' has been articulated is the diversity of reviewer responses to an article.

When the author(s) is unclear about the purpose and focus of the paper, each reviewer offers his or her own view about what direction to take the paper. When I hear young scholars complain that the reviewers are 'all over the place,' I surmise that part of the problem is that the purpose and intent of the author(s) is not clear.

Focusing on the 'take-away' is more important than one might think. Following this pattern helps the author(s) connect the dots in his or her own paper. Too often, authors write a conclusion that skitters away from the findings, drawing conclusions inadequately supported by the data. But, if in the conclusion the author states the original purpose and how that was accomplished, he ties himself to the scientific process specifically enough to resist going beyond the data. If there is any area where young scholars have not received enough training, it is in writing the conclusion of their research articles

How far do you go?
Scope and limitations

Many academics stumble over trying to articulate the purpose of the paper or proposal because they have not made up their own minds about how far they can go in pursuing their research question. This is often a flaw in their original research design. No one can answer all the related questions about an issue and stay focused, but they can acknowledge that those questions exist while they concentrate on a particular aspect. Such an approach dictates what is known as the 'scope' of the study, just as the scope of an instrument, such as a telescope, allows us to see only to a certain distance.

Take, for example, a paper exploring the effects of diet on health. The author, and the reader, will know that many other factors in a person's lifestyle affect health, such as exercise, stress, smoking, genetic predisposition, and so on. It is all too easy for an author who loses his or her focus on the original scope to follow through in detail the literature on the many other determinants of health. A focused researcher, on the other hand, would allude to the importance of the other factors, but explain that further detailed discussion of them is 'beyond the scope of this paper'. Continuing with the same example, rather than conduct research on each aspect of diet, the researcher is likely to have selected a single variable, such as food additives or protein intake, to study. The researcher has therefore narrowed the scope and must make a statement to that effect. Once again, they will not want to enter into a debate on the effects of all dietary influences but will make reference to one or two key works which have done so. Even within the chosen focus, such as food additives, a balance in a paper must be struck between existing research on the issue and the author's own findings. In this case, the author will take care to summarize the current body of knowledge to show the reader how they have taken it forward. Particularly when the paper is likely to challenge existing theory, the author must ensure that the reader knows that they are familiar with the assumed knowledge base.

If, for example, you were to study how to evaluate the effectiveness of training programmes in, say, the health service, you would have to confine yourself to the health service. You could not, however, approach that topic without first understanding the nature of training itself and how it is evaluated. In the same way, you would confuse your reader if you suddenly launched into health service training issues without first putting them in the picture.

Scholars frequently fear that what they are saying about one field, such as the effectiveness of training in the health service, will be criticized by others who might say that the same conclusions would not apply in, say, higher education. That fear can lead to a vagueness of purpose in the paper or proposal because the author tries to mask their lack of knowledge about wider application issues rather than meet that challenge head-on and state it. This can be accomplished by stating clearly that the scope of the research will be limited to the health service and suggesting that future studies on, say, training in the public sector as a whole, might build on and further the author's research. If there are implications for the wider field, these should be discussed as an implication, as we shall explore later.

Once the scholar clearly explains the scope, they can continue by acknowledging the related areas which have not been discussed but may be relevant. These can often be usefully cited by such phrases as: 'While it is beyond the scope of this paper/proposal to adequately cover the work on training evaluation in the private sector, readers are referred to the work of...'

Having defined the scope of the project, the researcher may either immediately or subsequently face constraints that affect the course of the study. These are commonly known as limitations. Time and money will limit the study, as will other constraints such as data availability. Some of these may not be evident at the beginning of the research but the researcher should demonstrate that they are aware of those possibilities, and consider how if they later arose, they affected the course of the research and validity of the findings.

The paper or proposal itself, being restricted by specified word counts, has limitations of its own, which again need explanation. Before beginning to refine the purpose statement of the paper or proposal, make sure you have noted the scope and limitations that will guide it. The following questions may help.

Scope: How far did I decide to look? What influenced that decision? What related issues did I not examine and why? Will I go on to examine those? Where can I guide the reader who wants to examine the related issues? To what extent can I generalize my conclusions?

Limitations: What constraints are imposed and why? Which are predictable? Which unexpected? How do they affect the validity of the study? How can future researchers, or I, vary them?

Authors usually find that once they have answered questions such as those above, they feel more confident about defining the purpose of the paper or proposal. Restrictions and limitations influence us, but do not necessarily reduce the contribution we make. The critical point is to be clear about what those restrictions are and tell the reader.

Context and literature review

Supporting concepts or evidence in a paper or proposal are critically important. The reviewer, and ultimately the reader, needs to know the difference between the author's concept and evidence and those of other contributors to the field. Yet, many authors do not know where to begin or where to stop referring to the work of others. Erring on the side of caution can lead to the absurd, with every idea or concept laboriously referenced to the point that any given paragraph simply reads as a stream of parentheses briefly interrupted by the author's words.

The way you treat the literature – indeed, the very reason why you read it in the first place – is also determined by the scope of the paper or proposal and should be clearly stated as such. This sets the context for your research. Whether you base the paper on a lengthier piece of work, such as a dissertation, or write it first as a paper, you will have surveyed other relevant works. In the same way, when preparing a proposal, you will have thought about how the work may fit into the wider body of knowledge and why your contribution is important. The criterion influencing how much literature to include in the paper relates to one word: requisite.

We have considered so far that authors are frequently criticized for not treating the literature in ways that are relevant to the question or helpful in providing insight into the body of knowledge. Of course, researchers normally rectify these problems during the course of academic research. Righting the wrongs will take more than revising a paper. If the core literature review is weak, it will be impossible to hide the flaws simply by writing well. What concerns us here is how to treat a good literature review for the purpose of communicating the salient points to the readers. You must therefore pay attention to the need to be thorough, relevant, and critical.

Being thorough means that you have read and evaluated the literature influencing the question. This is one of the factors which most affects the quality of papers and proposals. It is not possible to be thorough if you are not sure what the question is; this explains the weaknesses of many papers. That is why first defining your purpose, and then setting it within the appropriate context, is so important. Many authors frustrate their own efforts by allowing themselves to drift off on irrelevant tangents. Once again, being clear about the purpose and the implications eliminate this problem before it can start. The length of academic papers ranges between 3,500 and 12,000 words; a proposal's Case for Support may be between 3,000 and 5,000 words. Economy is therefore necessary if we are to retain the reviewer's, let alone the reader's, attention.

Try to imagine the background of the editor, reviewer, and the reader. Remember, many will be as familiar with the classic literature as you are. Their purpose in reading your paper or proposal is not to be reminded yet again about what everyone they have ever read has said before. They want to know what you are doing with what has been said. Failure to critically evaluate the literature and set the right context is a frequent criticism voiced by reviewers and by research student supervisors. If we apply the 'so what?' question here we can find that much of what we have been busy writing is not review but regurgitation.

Twenty words or less

Someone once said that if you cannot summarize your view of the world, your religion, or your philosophy in less than a minute, it is probably not worth saying. A weakness of many learned articles or research proposals is that the writer either had no clear idea of the paper's or proposal's purpose, or did, but did not know how to express it. Before going any further into planning your paper or proposal, make sure you know the answer to these questions:

- What do you want to say?
- Why should anyone care?

Why do you want to write the paper or do the research? We've already discussed some of the reasons, from the personal to the institutional perspective, in Chapters 2 and 3, but here we need to concentrate on the research or concept itself. The only purpose that is of interest to your reader is that your paper or proposal has something to say, and something to contribute. That 'something' is likely to include at least one or more from the following list.

- It adds conceptually to the current body of knowledge through new thinking.

- It adds empirically to the current body of knowledge through new evidence.
- It exposes a weakness in the current body of knowledge. It demonstrates a new way of applying the body of knowledge.
- It fixes a problem.

Implicit in all the above are the usual processes and standards you must apply. The research method must be robust, your literature review must be thorough and appropriate, your writing must be clear, and so on. But these alone are not enough. If your paper or proposal lacks purpose and implication, it will be just another routine review of either concept or evidence.

The first step is to write in 20 words or less your purpose in writing this paper or seeking research funding. These will not be necessarily the exact words used in the paper or proposal itself – although many would be improved by opening in just this way – but will help you clarify your own approach. You will revisit this purpose each time you consider a separate audience, to ensure that you modify the salient points for the benefit of your target group. We will discuss later how understanding the audience will help you position your work to make them relevant to different groups of readers. Any piece of research, however, will have begun with a purpose of some sort, either to prove, disprove, or extend. The following examples show how you might write a simple statement describing the purpose of your paper.

- 'I show how misinterpreting Smith's early work leads to wrong conclusions and weak hypotheses'
- 'I describe our evidence that molecular behaviour is not erratic in circumstances that others term chaotic'
- 'I provide new evidence linking customer service to internal team building'
- 'I produce a model to help evaluate poverty reduction programmes'

I am not proposing that your paper must open with a 20-word sentence, but that the act of creating such short statements will help provide your clear sense of purpose. An example from *The Canadian Geographer* shows the authors opening their paper by exploring key questions impacting on research into poverty and then clearly stating what their paper intends to explore:

It remains unclear whether the growth of the visible minority population (that mainly results from changes in the source countries of immigrants to Canada as well as higher birth rates among certain minority groups), has led to their spatial integration or segregation, and whether such spatial changes are linked to the patterning of high-poverty neighbourhoods.

(Walks and Bourne 2006)

It is clear from that example what the authors intend to show us and in what context it matters. If examples like these make it clear how important it is to focus, why do so many authors and research applicants find it difficult? Often, the obstacles relate more to confidence than context or content.

Fear of focus

Thus far we have seen how researchers state their purpose and have examined a few helpful techniques. Besides being unaware of these techniques, however, researchers sometimes have further reasons to resist clearly stating their intent. If we clearly state our purpose, we are leaving the reader in no doubt as to what we are going to say or do. That means we are going to actually have to say or do it. Worse, that means we can be criticized for not following through with the purpose. This criticism appears frequently on referees' reports, such as: 'Authors claim they are going to add new evidence to the body of knowledge … it's a pity they failed to do so.'

Why was that? Was the reviewer being too harsh? Fortunately, journal papers and funding proposals are rarely rejected for being bold or unconventional, or because a reviewer happens to hold an opinion other than the one you are expressing. Certainly, if you are proposing an idea that runs counter to the usual viewpoint in your field, you had best make sure your argument is sound. But your papers are only liable to incur the kind of comment above if you do not deliver the promise you made – and you cannot escape that promise.

A sense of purpose is crucial and fundamental. Editors reject papers that are vague and directionless. If what you have to say means you will be held to account for it, feel the fear, and do it anyway. Some people will agree with you, and some will not. But is that not the nature of philosophic enquiry? If we always simply supported the existing way of thinking, our field would wither and die. As a first step, ask yourself the following questions:

- Does my sense of purpose frighten me?
- What am I afraid of?
- Who am I afraid of?
- What's the worst that can happen if publish it?
- What's the worst that can happen if I do not?

Part of the fear of focus is one we have looked at in previous chapters – the fear of being imperfect. One way of overcoming the fear of imperfection is to be clear about your limitations and scope.

Finally, test out your purpose on other people. Make sure that anyone, including those not involved in your area of research, understands it. Make sure it is concise and to the point. Most importantly, make sure you can achieve it within the paper or the proposed research's timeline. It will act as your guide while you sketch out your outline and eventually choose the words to develop it.

I will now turn to more detail on writing research proposals. While the same principles as discussed above apply, the consistent attention to context, evaluation, and results require a closer look.

Writing clear research proposals

Each proposal, like every academic paper, is unique. You may be creating this as a reply to an invitation to tender, because you think your research matches a specific scheme or programme announced by the funder, or because it is your original idea and you want to pursue it. Alternatively, you may be submitting this after understanding a particular organization's issues, in which case this follows a lengthy exploration of someone's needs.

There is, therefore, no single 'right' way to write a proposal – no *pro forma* or standard structure which can be simply photocopied, filled in, and submitted. It will vary by funder. Nevertheless, every proposal, like every paper, shares certain characteristics. The purpose of this section is to summarize some of the key points which winning proposals appear to have in common. Remember, always, that there are equally good proposals flooding into your prospective funder's office every day.

When considering your proposal, look to see if it addresses the main issues:

- Research question
- Context
- Implications
- Method
- Outputs

Further, think about how to communicate those aspects. Think of what the ESRC says when it advises candidates in its guidance notes: 'Many proposals are unsuccessful not because they lack interesting or important research ideas, but because they fail to communicate adequately how these research ideas will be explored and translated into an achievable plan of action' (Economic and Social Research Council (ESRC) 2021).

The AHRC is equally clear. The best proposals respond to research questions concisely and with timescales. Not addressing them is the most common cause, according to the AHRC, of application failure. As they say in their guidance notes, applicants must outline clearly the 'rationale for the activities, approach and the research context in which they will operate'. Applicants are then guided to answering the following questions and headings in their accompanying Case for Support:

- What is the central theme of the proposed activity?
- Why is it important that this theme be explored?
- What is new and novel about the network?
- How will the questions be addressed?
- How will the proposed activities generate genuine and novel interaction across boundaries and so lead to advances in understanding?

The AHRC also advises in its guidance to applicants seeking follow-on-funding to be clear about the proposals' aims and objectives, and it is unequivocal about the consequences of not so doing: Applicants need to show how the project's aims and objectives will be met at specific stages in the project, as well as at completion. They need to demonstrate innovation, creativity, and engagement and 'proposals that fail to demonstrate this will not be considered for support, no matter how high the quality of the original research'.

Setting your research question

We have discussed earlier the importance of being clear about the nature of research questions and the need to focus. A former ESRC Research Director told me that 'The topic itself must be researchable. Sometimes it is such a large canvas that it is impossible to do.'

When Janet Lewis was Research Director of the Joseph Rowntree Foundation (the largest funder of social science research outside the research councils) she told me that sometimes, the research question is not only too large, but even unimportant or boring: 'You can have really good science on a really boring topic', she remarked. Focusing on the research question is hard work, she admits, but it is critical:

At one stage I started drawing up a kind of check list of important points, and one of them is, if the background and elaboration of the problem is longer than the methods and the aims, then it goes in the bin. This is a slight exaggeration, but I think there are, more seriously, two things. There's the kind of focus of the issue – does it fit into the priorities that we've identified? Have they addressed the issue? Quite a few people haven't really, because they're, not surprisingly, trying it on because they're desperate for money, so they will slightly modify what they want to do to try to fit into our brief, and it may not work. And then I think the other thing is how people are proposing to do the work and even though I think proposals have got better over the last few years, we still get an awful lot that are under-specified in terms of the method.

Context

The context referred to here is both the background of the research question and also the context of the funding partner and their community. It is important to understand who the partner is, who their stakeholders are, and how you fit into that community and can enrich it. In your proposal, you need to articulate that and make it clear to the funder that not only have you taken the time and effort to find out, but you know how to work within that context.

This book has referred to funders' guidance notes and websites. One of the interesting features of websites is that the owner can review and assess the navigation behaviour of those who visit it. Website owners review that kind of information frequently in an effort to improve their sites, but it is also used to get a better picture about the behaviour and characteristics of those who visit them. I heard from one research director that it is evident many researchers do not bother to find out enough about the organization: 'we know because we can see how far they have gone into our website. Many people do not go far enough.' Many academics just log on, download the application form, and log off.

It is important to demonstrate in your proposal that you have taken the trouble to find out who your funder is and how your proposed research matches their criteria. Some of your scrutinies will become obvious in the way that you frame your questions and situate them within the context. You can go further by using the actual language of the funder and referring to, for example, their strategic aims or points of ethos by quoting them directly. Do not just do the homework be seen to be doing it.

Method

Although this point has been dealt with in earlier chapters, it is worth repeating here as it is so often given as the primary reason for application failure. Describe your method in as much detail as possible. This is obvious, and yet often overlooked by poorly considered proposals. As mentioned earlier, lack of clarity about method is often the single most frequent cause of failure. Some applicants only offer a brief discussion of the subject area and a literature review. The methods must be appropriate and well-designed for the question, but simply mentioning that is not enough. Sufficient detail is necessary to convince the funder the methods have been designed and defined and the applicant knows how to carry them out. The majority of proposals which get close yet fail do so because research methods are either inappropriate or ill-defined. How can you be sure your proposal adequately covers method? Make sure it does not demonstrate:

- Vague research design and lack of clarity.
- Poor information about methods of data collection.
- Weak discussion of data analysis.
- Unrealistic timescales, often related to under-budgeting.

If, for example, you are proposing a quantitative survey, say what it will look like. If you are going to conduct focus groups, say why and how you will analyze them. Also, some experienced researchers assume that their experience alone will reassure the funder that they know how to collect and analyze data. Experienced as you may be, ensure you articulate this in your proposal as assessors may not be from your discipline or familiar with your background. The same advice applies to how much money you think you will need. Poor budgeting often results from poor consideration of method. Do you really think, for example, you can expect one research assistant to carry out six interviews a day for six months? Better to budget for two assistants than appear that you have not understood the implications of your research methods.

Many proposals which are well structured and thought-through may fail to convey the key points. This often happens when people try to write in a more complicated and supposedly sophisticated style than is necessary. Writing style is covered in much more detail in future chapters, and in particular in Chapter 11. For now, practise writing about your purpose as succinctly as possible until your friends, grandma, and teenage son can understand what you mean. They may not appreciate the finer detail, but they should grasp quickly what it is you intend to do.

In describing what your research is about it is useful to bear in mind the standard checklist given for story-writing in primary school:

- Who – is doing the research and for whom? How are they qualified to do it? Who are the readers/stakeholders/beneficiaries?
- What – is the paper/proposal about? What are its aims and objectives?
- Where – is it situated? By discipline, region, institution, as relevant.
- When – will/did it occur? At what stages? When will the results be realized?
- Why – is it important? This discipline/funder?
- How – will it or was it done? What challenges or lessons?

It is also worth remembering that a picture may indeed paint a thousand words. Many funders and successful researchers recommend using diagrams. This can quickly capture and convey important information.

Internal review

In order to check the clarity of your proposal, leave enough time to submit it for internal review in your institution. This may be organized by your central Research Services, or by your department, but ensure you engage in that process. As one research manager advises:

> Once you have written your case for support, you need to stand back from it. Academics are close to their work and sometimes forget that this is not an academic paper, but a sales pitch. Often, this doesn't come across.

This sometimes requires striking a fine balance between complying with the regulations of the external funder and meeting the academic's needs. Many academics under-estimate the role and potential of university research administrators. I advise people to be conscious of using your institution's internal review systems properly: research administrators can be highly valued colleagues in the successful submissions of proposals to funding bodies. While some academics refuse to admit that an administrator outside a subject area could possibly have anything useful to say about a proposal, they mistakenly ignore the fact that such people see more proposals and more responses from funding agencies in an average day than most academics see in years.

Summary

In this chapter, the two main critical success factors were discussed: purpose and implications. Although many academics find it difficult to stand back and look at their paper or proposal objectively, reviewers of journals and funding proposals see these two criteria clearly. That is why I recommend sharing papers and proposals with people outside one's own discipline, or even academia itself. Yes, you have written a few thousand elegant words, but 'so what?'.

Any paper or proposal needs to arrest the reader's attention by saying exactly what it is about, and why it is important.

Setting the research in context will reassure reviewers that a paper's or proposal's author knows where the research is situated, what has come before, and why this particular piece of research needs to be read about or funded.

Action points

Write down, in two or three sentences, the purpose of your planned paper or proposal. Start with the phrase 'The purpose of this paper/proposal is to…'. Consider verbs such as 'show', 'demonstrate', 'present', 'synthesize', 'explore', 'review', 'discuss', and 'identify'. Make sure you are explicit about what you are trying to do.

Then note how you are going to deliver the purpose: '… by illustrating with case examples…'; '… by describing the results of an experiment conducted…'; '… by reviewing the current literature on…' or, in the case of a proposal, by employing a specific method.

Finally, and preferably in the same paragraph or section, say why it is important.

Congratulations! You have just written one of your opening paragraphs! Remember, however, to revisit your purpose statement as you develop your paper or proposal to make sure it still promises what you are delivering.

References

Alon, Noga, Matias Yossi, and Szegedy Mario. (1999). 'The space complexity of approximating the frequency moments', *Journal of Computer and System Sciences*, 58: 137–147.

Economic and Social Research Council (ESRC) (2021). 'How to write a good proposal'. Available at: https://www.ukri.org/councils/esrc/guidance-for-applicants/how-to-write-a-good-proposal/

South African Journal of Economic and Management Sciences (n.d.). Submission Guidelines. Available at: https://sajems.org/index.php/sajems/pages/view/submission-guidelines

Walks, Alan R., and Larry S. Bourne (2006). 'Ghettos in Canada's cities? Racial segregation, ethnic enclaves and poverty concentration in Canadian urban areas', *The Canadian Geographer/Le Géographe canadien*, 50: 273–297.

7   SO WHAT?
Implications

Why is it important?

As discussed in the previous chapter, the most important criteria for a paper or proposal's success are that the purpose and implications are clear. Although I touched on this in the previous chapter, implications are so important that I will break the concept down here into smaller segments relating to specific parts of a paper or proposal and look at it from multiple perspectives. Implications are embedded in many, if not all, of a research project.

Unfortunately, academics frequently bridle at being told, as they are increasingly, that their research needs to have 'impact'. Too often, they assume that 'impact' is something that needs to be described in monetary terms, but that is not always the case. The impact of one's research may, indeed, be felt quantitatively in society, but it can also be felt qualitatively: increasing government understanding of social inequalities, for example, or moving one's discipline forward through your research are both examples of 'impact'.

As we become immersed deeply in a piece of research it is easy to lose sight of its value for others who are not as familiar with the area. Even people working on the same problem may not have been privy to your approach and findings, until the article appears. The implications of what you have done may be obvious to you, but will they be obvious to anyone else? Who is better placed to predict the impact of your research than you?

Many researchers, even experienced authors, find it difficult to step back and look at their work from the reader's perspective. The reasons for this are varied but may often be the same concerns that confronted us when considering publishing or applying for funding at all: fear of judgement and the need for perfection.

Stating the implications of research is the moment when we crystallize the value of our work. This can be a disconcerting experience, for we are boldly setting out in black and white what we believe that other people should think about the work we have done or intend to do. Would it not

DOI: 10.4324/9781003259718-8

it be easier, and less unnerving, to let them draw their own conclusions? Easier, perhaps, but only in the short term. A paper or proposal lacking clear implications will usually be rejected or sent back for revision. My analysis of referees' reports and discussions with editors, authors, funders, and successful applicants make it clear that the implications factor is the criterion, following 'purpose', that transcends all others.

We may, for example, create a reasonable literature review, proper research design, detailed and appropriate method, readability, and so on, all of which are important, but are considered as only the entry point for a good academic paper or proposal. We need to move further. This is how one reviewer expressed it: 'Presented some facts and shown some differences but has not shown that these findings are important.'

That is the type of work that might be expected from an undergraduate approaching a subject for the first time and needing to summarize what the relevant thinkers have written so far. There may even be a section describing something the author has observed but which he or she has so far not thought to interpret and analyze. It leads the reviewer to read the paper, shrug their shoulders, and ask, 'So what?'

Another reviewer commented:

> I would regard this as the application of existing theory to a stated problem – a consultancy type assignment. The paper is quite theoretical. It reads OK with little amendment. However, it is of limited application and I doubt whether you would wish to publish it.

Although we may fear that readers will disagree with our statement about our work's value, probably the biggest obstacle is, once more, our need to be perfect. We must appreciate the reader or reviewer as someone whose interest in our work may only be peripheral, or who may even be a student approaching the subject for the first time. We may know that our research in the field is continuing and that more answers will arise in the future, but where does that leave the reader or reviewer?

It may help to consider that point more fully, thereby easing our concern that the work may be as yet unfinished. A publishable paper must encapsulate the essence of what we have done thus far and draw out conclusions even as we stand on a moving line. Try to view it as a milestone, if not the end point. Explaining that to your readers will reassure both you and them that you have not yet reached the end of the line, but that significant implications are arising *en route*. A funding proposal can be clear about the work that needs to be done now, and also what will remain to be done.

At funding workshops I have organized worldwide, the discussion around 'impact' provokes more concern, and cynicism, than any other topic. Many academics erroneously feel that funders are unfairly applying pressure on them to commercialize or in other ways make money from their research. But money-making is not the definition of Impact. Funders have specific notes about what they consider impact to mean, so it is vital that you check their own guidelines. The UK's largest funder of social science research, the Economic and Social Research Council (ESRC), is clear that (Economic and Social Research Council (ESRC) 2021) 'impact' can mean both quantitatively measurable economic effects as well as intangible academic results, such as 'shifting understanding and advancing scientific method, theory and application across and within disciplines'.

While 'impact', according to many funders, needs to be understood in terms of economic and societal impact on individuals, organizations, and/ or the nation. Sometimes, impact is measured in terms of its efficacy and urgency. A call for 'Action-Lebanon' (agence nationale de la recherche (anr) 2021) projects, for example, was aimed specifically at 'supporting urgent, rapid and structuring research projects, of a maximum duration of 18 months, whose scientific relevance is related to the COVID-19 pandemic and to the recent multi-dimensional crises that occurred at a very critical period in Lebanon's history'. The research programme, managed jointly by Lebanese and French governments, looked for research to:

> assess and analyze the impact of the COVID-19 pandemic on the different human, social, economic, environmental and health aspects, and propose mechanisms to reduce vulnerability and strengthen Lebanese resilience in all categories (scientific, health, social, economic, psychological, etc.).

In this case, as the Call noted, 'Issues related to risk assessment and management, direct and indirect impact analysis, and remediation are therefore key.'

Impact can therefore take many forms, as the ESRC describes, to include:
- Instrumental impact – influencing the development of policy, practice, or services; shaping legislation; and changing behaviour.
- Conceptual impact – contributing to the understanding of policy issues and reframing debates.
- Capacity building through technical and personal skill development.

While expanding the idea of 'impact' is instructive, it is also useful to make sure you ask yourself the question – matters to whom? The ESRC, for example, has an annual award to recognize those who, in their estimation, have succeeded in making impacts. The 'Celebrating Impact Prize', open to ESRC-funded researchers recognizes that impact can be felt in several ways:

- Outstanding Business and Enterprise Impact
- Outstanding Public Policy Impact
- Outstanding Societal Impact
- Outstanding International Impact
- Outstanding Early Career Impact

In 2020 the prize was awarded to Prof. Arjan Verschoor and Prof. Ben D'Exelle because of their funded work to help farmers in Uganda. As discussed in Chapter 2, the researchers worked for two decades to improve farming in Uganda. A major impact was felt through the unique UAIS that was created because of the research.

Implications within the research proposal or paper can appear in several sections, not just the overall consideration of the project's 'impact' as a whole. Next, we will consider implications within the research-related literature or academic context.

Implications with a paper or proposal

One question new authors frequently ask is: 'How much of a review of the literature do I need to put in?' The answer is 'just enough'. The next question, of course, is 'Well, so how much is enough?' for which the answer is again enigmatic, if not totally unhelpful 'It depends.' The quantity of the literature review is defined by the original research question, the scope of the paper or proposed project, and by the author's evaluation of the literature.

There are no rules about how many references a given paper or proposal needs: some have only a few, others have many. Editors and reviewers all know how easy it is to add names to a reference list; authors seeking to impress with the length, rather than the relevance, of their list of references are therefore unlikely to succeed. Particularly with the accessibility of online databases, bulking a reference list has never been easier, or potentially less meaningful. An editor or referee seeking to assess the quality of the literature review or survey will formulate three principal questions:

1. Does it reflect the purpose of the paper or proposal?
2. Does it match the scope of the paper or proposal?
3. What are its implications?

In this section I will concentrate on how to ensure that you are able to draw out the implications of literature and scope, how the use of the literature reflects the purpose and scope, and what you must do to answer the 'so what?' questions. First, I will examine how the scope affects the choice of literature. Second, I will show how to evaluate the literature properly to interest and guide the reader.

Scope – how much is enough?

I examined in the previous chapter the concept of scope through examining purpose; therefore, the nature of scope and how to describe it for the reader should now be familiar concepts. The reader needs to know, no more nor less, what the key assumptions are of your paper or proposal. You should therefore provide that knowledge where statements or evidence are questionable or controversial.

If, for example, you are setting out to disprove a strongly held theory, then the reader will want to know exactly whose theory is being disputed. If you want to demonstrate how an accepted theory can be applied in a new setting, then the reader will again want to know what the original theory is. There will often be several tangential issues relating to any theory, and while authors and applicants may want to follow all those routes in an effort to enlighten the reader completely, there will neither be space nor time. It may help to think about the implications of your choices by asking the following questions:

- Is that requisite knowledge?
- Is it necessary, and does it relate closely to the scope of the paper or proposal?
- Are you able to answer 'so what?' by showing how the literature thus far needs correction, improvement or addition?

Such care avoids the likelihood of prompting the following reviewer comment:

> Author writes on a subject upon which there has been a lot of debate. It would have been appreciated had he or she demonstrated an awareness of this.

It may help in this context to imagine the scope of the paper as a river, whose banks confine your research. Various tributaries and streams join and issue from the river and connect to related areas that could be followed but lie outside your focus. Identify these for your reader but resist the temptation to follow them all in your current paper or proposal.

Implications of the literature

Work on the assumption that the journal reviewers reading your paper have read it all before. Many may be more familiar than are you with works on the subject. Not only have they read the key writers in the original, but they have also sifted through hundreds of papers that discuss them. They have probably heard thousands of undergraduates summarize the principal theories and many of their related strands. Indeed, if they read one more treatise about what everybody famous has already said about the subject, they would fall asleep.

That you have compiled yet another 'who's who' in the field will not interest your potential reader either. There are, however, occasions when drawing together the literature will have implications for the reader. Two examples in particular will have impact:

- This is a field in which no one has previously drawn together related thoughts on the subject.
- This is a field where you alone have discovered that other researchers have got it wrong.

If your paper falls into either of the above two categories, congratulations. Your paper will indeed contribute greatly to the body of knowledge and fire the imagination of your reviewers and readers. Your only problem will be in keeping within your scope and supporting fully your claims that you are truly original. These sorts of papers, which are essentially literature reviews in themselves, are both exceptional and valuable to scholars everywhere.

Summarizing the field, however original the scope, does not eliminate the need to explain the implications. For papers and for proposals, you must still describe what the reader might do next. In most cases, you will accomplish this by indicating the areas for further research, or areas where existing research needs to be re-examined. As a result, you will usefully provide or propose a new framework for an emerging body of knowledge. Students and researchers will benefit from finally having a clear picture of the new field and its antecedents. They will be able to learn from that and build upon it. Although you are not claiming original research, you are making sense for the first time of what has gone before and indicating where researchers might go next.

In the second instance, you may be able to point out why research in a given field may be going in the wrong direction. Many researchers may be working on the assumptions of other researchers that you are now able to point out are wrong. The flaws in the existing body of knowledge are exposed, and you are helping other researchers by leading them away from blind alleys. In that case, you must take pains to explain the key points which are being criticized.

More than ever, you must retain full attention on the scope. An author who is starkly refuting existing theories will be subject to close scrutiny by reviewers and readers, some of whom may want to defend the theories in question and will look for any reason, however small, to discredit the author or applicant. Moving away from the point may reveal weaknesses on related topics to use against the author, even if they are not entirely relevant. The message here is: hold your ground and resist the temptation to wander. The fewer steps in a process or argument, the more likely it is to deliver what it should. Do not make the mistake of confusing quality with complexity.

Evaluate – don't regurgitate

Other than the examples noted above, most authors and applicants will be using the literature to help the reader understand the context of their research. As explained earlier, you should strenuously avoid behaving like a third-year student writing an essay on what everyone else has said. When writing a research proposal, however, you must assume that some reviewers will not be experts in your area, and you will therefore need to explain clearly the literature that has come before and why your proposed research is necessary.

Many reviewers look first at the list of references to assess quickly whether the author is drawing upon recent, or previously neglected, authors. Do not provide a reference list with all the usual names from earlier decades, generated without reference to what people were saying and why it is important in the context of your paper. You will only be demonstrating to the reviewer immediately that you are simply rehashing the obvious. In most cases, this would disqualify it as a publishable paper in a reputable journal and would reduce the impact of a research proposal: the reviewer's only conceivable reaction in this case would be: 'So what?'

As a consistent rule of thumb, check your own references for a balance between old and new. Ask yourself if you have explored fully the implications of original or foundational works, or are you reporting on them parrot-fashion? Before taking for granted that the theories still stand, have you reviewed what more recent authors are saying about the standard theories? There is little point in blithely referring to the well-accepted theories of 'Professor So-and-So' if, during the last year, recent research has seriously challenged or even invalidated her work. Consider also when using current sources whether the authors have correctly identified their sources. As ever, the original scope will dictate how extensively you need to report on the work of other researchers.

Apart from simply tacking on a few references to support the key points, authors must be able to evaluate the literature. Editors send many papers back because the author was unable to move beyond merely describing what they had read. Funders may be perplexed about how a proposal would move the field forward. Such a paper caused one reviewer to comment:

> This paper reads more like an undergraduate essay than a serious article for an academic/professional journal. … Although it reviews quite a large literature, most of the works receive only a very superficial mention. There is little attempt to integrate or critically evaluate earlier published work on the subject.

What can we learn about the reviewer's exhortation to integrate and critically evaluate earlier published works? Many supervisors direct their students to follow several steps when conducting an evaluative literature review. This, eventually, helps the student realize that a review itself is only a first step. The sequence I devised to help students remember how to evaluate is:

Summarize $\rightarrow$ synthesize $\rightarrow$ analyse $\rightarrow$ authorize

Summarize

This is just the first step in a literature review but is also, unfortunately, where most people stop. Who are the key contributors to the field of enquiry and what did they individually say of significance? As readers will note, answering this question is impossible if our scope is as yet ill-defined or you have allowed yourself to drift away from it. Whether or not we want to summarize each author or move straight on to the next step depends on both the scope and the audience. Are we attempting to pull apart contributions made thus far so that we may criticize them? In that case, we will have to summarize the key findings of each person first. If, however, we are trying to provide a quick overview of past work so that our readers can now see our findings in context it will be more important to synthesize rather than summarize.

Synthesize

Following a summary of key concepts, we need to draw out the implications for our reader by making sense of where the past has brought us. We might choose to synthesize the literature using a chronological model that shows how one person's theory was enriched by the next person, before another person later extended it, and so on. Or we might synthesize according to a key theme we are investigating, bringing together other authors' work under the themes, questions or problems we are currently exploring.

Analyze

Through analysis, the author critically evaluates previous work. At that time, they will be highlighting contributions or flaws influencing their own research, if not the body of knowledge as a whole. The scope for the evaluation is the question being pursued and the author's findings, or proposed research, relating to it. This step can only follow the previous two steps. Literature cannot be analyzed without first summarizing key stages in its evolution and making sense of, or synthesizing, its current position.

Authorize

At some point in the paper or proposal, the author or applicant will describe their own findings or intentions in light of the critical evaluation of the literature. The authorization may be in support of previous works, or it may be authorizing the author's or applicant's own view opposing the literature thus far. This is the final and critical stage of the paper or proposal, for having looked at the literature, made sense of it and analyzed it, the author or applicant must extend the body of knowledge, purposefully depart from it, or show how it will be remedied or supplemented.

When authors or applicants fail to put their stamp on the body of knowledge, the reviewers mutter, 'So what? Here you have described where everyone else is, told me what you have done, yet not made any connection between the two.' It is the moment of connection between the published past and the present or future that gives the reader the whole picture of the author's or applicant's work or proposal. It is the final and most conclusive implication an author or applicant can share, yet it is one which many authors or applicants resist, for reasons discussed in previous chapters.

Former journal editor Marie Cornwall (2010) recalled that when she was editor she would ask reviewers considering a paper to answer yes or no to the question: 'Does the paper make a substantial theoretical contribution?' Unfortunately, she recalled, the answer was 'no' nine times out of ten: 'submissions are often most lacking in this area', she wrote.

Not answering the 'so what' question related to theory may happen for several reasons, she explained. The author may not have situated the work explicitly at the outset, and therefore did not know which areas could represent a significant contribution. Or, an author might have tried to refute or extend an existing theory, but does so incorrectly. This reveals their ignorance about the field itself or its direction. Another problem is when an author is merely descriptive, reporting on empirical findings and perhaps some correlations, but only making conclusions about those findings. Authors need to return to the theoretical points that arose earlier, and respond to those:

> Thus, the paper does not contribute to theory building because in the end the focus of the authors is on whether variable A predicts variable B, having neglected the original purpose of the paper. [...] authors should discuss the empirical findings and then fully discuss the implications of the findings for the theory that guided the research.

Cornwall points out that her comments apply equally to authors of qualitative or quantitative articles. Each needs to move beyond the descriptive level and tackle 'the more difficult task of taking descriptive knowledge (correlations, associations, and odds ratios in quantitative research, and descriptions of social processes in qualitative research) and translating it into theoretical insight'.

Implications are not reiterations

When considering the implications of your work, try to identify and articulate the worth of your work to others. This is making good the promise you made at the beginning of the article or proposal when you stated your purpose. Concluding the section with a summary of findings is not the same as pointing out the impact of your work and how it will affect others. If you have contributed or propose to contribute to the body of knowledge through new conceptual thinking, what will it matter? How have you contributed? How will you? Why should anyone care? How will they be able to use what you have discovered? If you have applied current thinking to a new area, or intend to, what can anyone do about it? How will your work change anything in thought or practice? What, specifically, do further researchers or practitioners need to do next?

The implications of your work may be for research or practice, but they must be described. It is not your reader's job to try to decode what your significant message may be. You should say, clearly and in full, what you believe the implications of your analysis are to others. As we well know, the problem today in most fields is not a lack of information but a vast, often vague, morass of information through which we must painstakingly sieve. The better journals, and therefore the better authors, are those which cut through the sieving process for the readers and bring them straight to the point. The same applies to the funding proposals most likely to succeed. As a reader, we may choose to agree, to disagree, to adapt an author's ideas, to ignore them, or to follow them. That is up to us. Those responsible for judging those articles or proposals and bringing them from author to reader or funder understandably become a little impatient with anything less than a straight answer to the obvious question: 'So what?'

One of the most difficult tasks is to ask yourself why the work will apply to a broader audience in your discipline. It is easy to become so focused on your own research that you fail to connect what you are doing with what other people are doing.

Dr Ian Woodward lectured in sociology in the School of Arts, Media and Culture at Griffith University when I interviewed him. He had just won the Best Paper award in the *Journal of Sociology* for his paper 'Divergent narratives in the imagining of the home amongst middle-class consumers Aesthetics, comfort and the symbolic boundaries of self and home' (Woodward, 2003). When I asked him why he thought his paper had been recognized as 'best', he said he thought he had succeeded in being able to draw out the implications from his micro, fieldwork-based study and apply them in a wider context.

> Especially when you are writing for generalist journals in your field (e.g., the *Journal of Sociology* etc.) you must draw out the implications of your research for larger or enduring questions in your discipline. Of course this must be done in a balanced and appropriately modest way but it is important to situate your research within a bigger disciplinary picture.

Particularly when research is small-scale and ethnographic in nature, authors must work hard to generalize findings for a broader audience. He adds:

> This is especially relevant when you are undertaking research that is mi-cro in nature: if it doesn't link to broader questions then readers may consider it too local and without larger implications. This means it won't be published or if it is it may be unlikely to be cited in the future. I suppose part of the skill here is in telling a story or narrative (within aca-demic and scholarly conventions) about the importance of your research

A statement of implications gives us a way to generalize our findings. Re-search that only applies to you personally in your own precise situation can be of no value to anyone else. One criterion for being published or funded is that authors must contribute to the body of knowledge. They must show why their research matters. What are the steps that we need to take to accomplish this?

Implications of the research process

As I discussed in Chapter 3, applicants for funding in particular need to be sure about their research process and understand the difference between the research process and the research problem. This is particularly important if the author mentions in the introduction why and how the research is important for others. If it is a problem that needs resolution, relating to a wider issue in the general body of knowledge, so what? Have you discovered anything that should be applied or understood by others? What are the implications of this particular research problem resolution, and what are the implications for the body of knowledge on the redefined issue?

Scholars writing for academic journals need to be aware of this as well. One author who had not met these criteria caused a reviewer to comment:

> Introductory section is poorly structured, lacking clear problem definition. Conclusions could tie in more fully to some of the issues raised in the introduction.

The research problem is, however, not the whole story. No researcher can investigate a problem without understanding the context. These are the issues that enclose the problem. The implication will therefore relate to the issue itself and may give direction to other researchers in light of the new findings from the specific research.

Having properly identified the problem and issue, the research design then includes a method by which the research will gather relevant data. What are the implications of that method? Are there implications simply for the particular researcher, or are they for others in the field? What, for example, are the implications of face-to-face interviews as opposed to questionnaires? What are the implications of a double-blind controlled trial? Why did the author or applicant choose a certain data-gathering technique rather than any other, and what limitations and implications may arise as a result?

Once we have the data, we need to make sense of what we have found by turning data into intelligence. This is where we apply the data to the original question and analyze it. But, once again, we need to explain the implications of any analytical method we have chosen, for the process by which we interpret the data will determine how we make sense of it. Readers or reviewers may disagree with our interpretation and be at a loss to know how we arrived at our own conclusions unless we tell them.

Finally, our analysis or 'findings' should lead us to a resolution of the problem in a way that makes sense for our readers. It is at this stage we will draw out, or propose to draw out, the implications of our analysis to resolve the problem and to add further to the existing body of knowledge on the issue.

Returning to the paper cited in the previous chapter about Canadian urban poverty, the authors concluded that:

> research examined here suggests that the confluence of increasing income inequality and the particular geography of housing in each given place, including that of tenure, form and price, are more important in determining overall patterns of segregation.
>
> (Walks and Burns 2006)

It is now clear what the authors found and why it matters.

As we have seen, implications cannot casually be left as an afterthought in the last 200 words. As implied in the referee's statement earlier, an ill-considered introduction which takes no account of implications will cause problems later. Implications must direct the paper or proposal from the beginning of the research process.

Articulating implications

Knowing your implications helps you decide what should be included in your paper or proposal and what can be omitted. Particularly if you are writing about a lengthy piece of research, you will be distilling detailed and important work into only a few thousand words. How do you know what is important and what is not? The only way to answer that question is to be certain which essential points you must cover to convey the value of your research to readers.

The first step, as discussed earlier, is to define your purpose. Naturally following from that is to articulate the implications of the research:

Step 1: Purpose. What is it and why does it matter?
Step 2: Implications. This is why it matters and to whom.

An extract from Dr Woodward's award-winning paper can serve as an excellent example:

> This article does not seek to challenge this core notion in the sociology of consumption, but seeks a corrective that addresses the ways in which narrative, symbolic boundaries and practices of consumption constitute such cultural forms. This corrective is necessary because, while the theoretical terrain within consumption studies has more recently shifted towards freedom, expressivity and identity in explaining consumption (as reviewed by Warde, 1997), relatively little empirical scholarly inquiry has been directed toward an understanding of the strategies and practices of individual consumers within particular consumption domains sensitive to the accomplishment of these narratives.
>
> (Woodward 2003, 392)

It is clear how he has put himself in the reader's mind, considering questions that might occur to someone interested in the outcomes of the research.

Key questions can be asked here:

- What wider principles emerged from your research?
- How can people in your field use it?
- Can people in other fields use it?
- How can other researchers take your work forward?
- How can your research be applied in practice?

The answers to some of these questions may be 'don't know' or 'not applicable'. Which ones do apply, and what are your answers?

Finding more

Having tackled the most important guides to implications – purpose, context and findings – try to look at the various components of your paper or proposal and articulate further their implications. Each decision you have made needs to be explained. Implications in the literature are so important that I have devoted considerable space to writing a literature review with evaluative and analytical techniques which can help your reader. There are, however, many other sections of a paper or proposal that also have implications:

- What were the implications of your scope and limitations?

- What were the implications of choosing particular methods of data gathering and analysis?
- Did, or will, certain techniques cast some doubts or further veracity on your findings?

Prepare yourself a list of answers to the questions that might arise about the effect of your approach. Try to work out the implications not only of your significant findings but also the impact that your approach has had on the project itself and your conclusions.

Implication checklist

- *Purpose.* What is it and why does it matter?
- *Findings.* Why, for whom, and how do they matter?
- *Literature.* What did it say and how does it matter to your research?
- *Methodology.* How did it or will it affect the findings?
- *Analysis.* How did the techniques affect, or will affect, your findings?
- *Options.* What are the implications of potential answers to the problem?
- *Conclusion.* How far are you prepared to go and why?

As an exercise, take a few moments to note down, in 20 words or less, answers to the above questions. If you find this difficult, you will need to think longer and harder before approaching your paper or proposal. Once you have condensed your implications into 20 words or less you will be better able to review your work and decide what is important.

At least we may be able to avoid the sting of another reviewer who wrote:

> The 'surprising result' would not have been particularly surprising if the authors had thought at the beginning of the study what they had expected to find.

Implementing implications

As discussed in Chapter 3, research may lead to a number of outcomes. The example quoted there from the SSRC showed how that funder expressed such possibilities, particularly in terms of collaborative activities and public-facing initiatives.

The idea of 'public facing' may worry academics who are more accustomed to communicating with peers, who already understand similar ideas, theories and methods than someone from the 'general public'. One way into this process is to recognize that few research projects are of apparently mass interest. It is important to understand your audience – a theme I turn to in more depth in the following chapters.

Whether research has implications for further research, immediate practice or both, consider carefully how the reader can use this knowledge in practice. Although your initial reaction might be that such direction lies outside the scope of the paper, who is in a better position than the original author to suggest how the reader might proceed further?

If we think through the point made earlier in this chapter, that the author or applicant is often someone who is continuing research, what specific steps are being laid out for other researchers or practitioners? Consider, for example, the reader as a PhD student reading the article and interested in taking some of the points further. By telling the reader how to do something useful with the findings, the author is making a chain for someone else to follow. What are the links in that chain?

When considering the useful outcomes of your research, run through the who, what, where, when and how questions that might provoke some answers or at least strong hints to give your readers: Who is able to apply your findings? What might they do? When and where might it be done? How might they approach it? Too often, we leave the follow-through to our reader's imagination. Given our intense involvement in the question at hand, we ought to be able to offer more than an offhand 'go away and think about it' statement.

All of the above means that authors or applicants must think through implications carefully before they even begin to think about writing. We need to view the meaning of our work from our readers' perspectives and let that permeate the entire paper. Otherwise, we are just offering our reader something upon which to ruminate, and everyone, particularly our reader, is too busy sifting through too many papers to bother with that. Both funding proposals and papers need to build in from the beginning statements about they the research is important.

Before moving on, make notes in answer to some of the questions listed above. Don't worry yet at this stage whether you have exactly the right words. There will be plenty of time to polish your writing. For now, just see if you can identify what really matters about your paper, or proposal, to whom, and why. As always, it may be a good idea to review these short points with a colleague not completely familiar with your area. Read out your statements of purpose, followed by the key implications of your findings. Do they match? Go through some of the decisions you have made and explain briefly the implications of each. Do they satisfy? Encourage him or her to question you with what are probably the most illuminating words in the scholarly publishing vocabulary – 'So what?'

In the end, you will be delivering the promise of insight and relevant implications you made to your reader or reviewer who has patiently stayed with you for a few thousand words just to find out more detail. At the very least, you do not wish to frustrate the reader or reviewer: at best, you want him or her to finish the article or proposal knowing that it was of value.

Summary

During the preceding five chapters I have explored the paper from the author's point of view, reminding ourselves about why we should publish, and why sometimes we feel we shouldn't. On making a closer analysis, we have found that even good research is not communicated if the paper has no purpose or implications. Next, we will be turning the mirror round and reflecting on the world of the editor, reviewer, and reader. What we will see is a different point of view entirely. For many aspiring or new authors or applicants, it will be an unfamiliar world, a place of mystery and arcane knowledge. And yet, the reality is very different. Editors, reviewers, and readers are not, after all, formidable or forbidding. They're just people like you.

Action points

Note down the key reference sources in your paper or proposal. Next to each one, make a short note about why you are referencing it. What value does it add? Look at the publication dates. How many are more than five years old? How many are less than two years old?

Now, draft a few paragraphs dealing with one of the aspects of the literature you are reviewing. Do not worry about spending too much time polishing them: just put them down in draft form. Check whether you have summarized (briefly captured the relevant key points of each of your cited authorities), synthesized (brought together any threads), analyzed (brought the section to a relevant and logical conclusion), and authorized (put your own stamp upon it).

Action points

The following exercise will make sure that no one will read your paper or proposal and say, 'So what? Now what?' Write a paragraph which sets out, clearly and explicitly, what a member of the general public, with no background in your field, would make of your paper or your proposed project. Put yourself in your reader's place for a moment.

Now write another paragraph doing the same for a researcher in your field. You have gained from other researchers by picking up a link of a chain and using it in your research. Make a new link, so the chain can be passed on. Suggest some areas for further research. Remind readers of the limitations and scope of your work.

Congratulations again! Now you have one of your most important paragraphs. As you write your paper, keep reviewing your implications. These are what your readers will take away with them.

References

agence nationale de la recherche (anr) (2021). 'Call for projects Action-Lebanon'. Available at: https://anr.fr/en/call-for-proposals-details/call/call-for-projects-action-lebanon/

Cornwall, Marie (2010). 'From the editor: Ten most likely ways an article submission fails to live up to publishing standard', *Journal for the Scientific Study of Religion*, 49(4): i–v.

Economic and Social Research Council (ESRC) (2021). 'Defining impact'. Available at: https://webarchive.nationalarchives.gov.uk/ukgwa/20211020025046/; https://www.ukri.org/councils/esrc/impact-toolkit-for-economic-and-social-sciences/defining-impact/

Walks, R. Alan and Larry S. Bourne (2006). 'Ghettos in Canada's cities? Racial segregation, ethnic enclaves and poverty concentration in Canadian urban areas', *The Canadian Geographer/Le Géographe canadien*, 50: 273–297.

Woodward, Ian (2003). 'Divergent narratives in the imagining of the home amongst middle-class consumers: Aesthetics, comfort and the symbolic boundaries of self and home', *Journal of Sociology*, 39: 391–412.

PART II

KNOWING YOUR AUDIENCE

8 CHOOSING THE RIGHT PUBLISHER OR FUNDER

Finding the right journal

Many novice academics are unaware of one of the most important aspects of their publishing strategy: anything they send to a journal must be original. As I discussed in Chapter 1, that consideration must form part of your publishing strategy. This means that if in the haste to be published following a PhD you have published your thesis as a book, you have likely harmed your chances of being published in a top journal. And, considering that for prestige, international reputation, job prospects and promotion, journals are more highly related than books, this could have been a serious setback.

In any case, it is important for any academic's career to secure publication in one or more academic journals. But which ones?

That question has become more complicated during the last decade, and particularly since I wrote the first edition of *How to Get Published in Journals* in 1996 and revised it ten years later in 2006. While the general principles held, and still do, an important development has been the pervasive practices of digital publishing, Today's new academics have likely never physically held a journal in their hands. They do not know that a journal is like a book, with each 'issue' containing seven to ten 'chapters', known as 'papers', not articles. These papers are selected for publication after a rigorous and lengthy editorial review process and, most likely, at least one revision by the author following detailed feedback from the reviewers and editors. The papers chosen for any one issue are selected by an editor or editorial team – and we will explore more about them in the next chapter. Each issue belongs to a year's work of publication known as the 'volume'. There may be two to 12 issues in any one volume.

New academics will likely never see any one issue in its entirety, or certainly not any one volume with its issues neatly stacked together along a library shelf. They will see a paper for the first time as part of a university course where it appears on a reading list. This change in experience has an

DOI: 10.4324/9781003259718-10

important consequence: new academics do not have a picture, physically or mentally, of the 'journal' but see individual papers disaggregated from the whole, seemingly floating in a digital space on its own. But crucially, it is not on its own and it is not floating. It is deeply connected to other papers in the same journal and embedded in discourse, regulations, norms, conversations, processes, expectations, standards, personalities, and histories unique to that journal. Being published in *that* journal means being a part of *that* whole. How, then, can you as a new academic determine if that 'whole' is where they want to be? Will it be the right fit? Is that where you want to be seen, or be read? Do the people you want to reach – colleagues, more senior academics, potential funders – also read that journal? And how will you manage to convince the editors, the gatekeepers, to accept you? Those are tough questions and big challenges. And, unfortunately, the failure rate is high.

One of the world's leading publishers, Elsevier, conducted research into publication success rates across a range of journals, not only their own (Elsevier n.d.). They found that, on average, the 'acceptance rate' was 32 per cent. The same report helpfully included information about the variability of the term 'acceptance rate'. Some journals may calculate this by simply dividing the number of papers submitted by the number published, when others might consider instead the numbers that actually made it into the review process.

Of the *bona fide* journals they researched, they found broad, and useful, comparisons: larger journals have lower acceptance rates than smaller journals, but with considerable variation (between 5 and 60 per cent) and high-impact journals have a lower acceptance rate, but with considerable variation (from 5 to 50 per cent).

They also note that a high acceptance rate may be related to the so-called 'predatory journals' that purport to be academic, and therefore a sensible place to publish, when in fact they are unscrupulous businesses that charge high publication rates in order simply to make money. This worrying trend was reviewed in detail in Chapter 1, and to recap here, remember: avoiding the scam of predatory journals is straightforward, and links to all the points described below about how to target a journal. Just keep in mind: if you and your colleagues have never heard of a journal that is making an unsolicited approach to you, bin it. They only succeed because new scholars have not yet understood that a journal is a community, a conversation, and a part of an existing academic record.

Now, back to acceptance rates: how can you improve your chances? The main criterion is to ensure you are submitting your paper to the right journal. Many editors say that many of the manuscripts they receive do not even reach the review stage. They are immediately rejected because they do not meet the editorial objectives of the journal. This is what an editor of the leading science journal *Nature* said when I interviewed her about submissions to that esteemed journal:

> When we receive a manuscript, we decide whether to send it for peer review on the basis of its suitability for *Nature* (novel, of broad general interest, arresting, a clear conceptual advance, free of obvious flaws, well written). Of the manuscripts, between half and a quarter are sent for review.

That means between half and three quarters are not sent for review. Papers are rejected even before they are assessed for scientific content mainly because the author has not even met the most basic criterion necessary: is this the right community? Talking to other editors over the years, I found that the *Nature* case is not unusual. On average, about half of all submissions are rejected immediately. This section is about how to reduce the chances of that happening to you. To begin, we need to ensure that those who will assess your paper actually get to read it.

Few journals in the academic field are bought in large numbers. Many focus so tightly on a particular *niche* that they will only be of interest to a few thousand, or even a few hundred, institutions. Whether or not people renew their subscriptions depends on whether they are satisfied with the journal. That means the journal must continue to appeal to its target audience. The appeal will come, not from the cover design or even the respected names on the advisory board, but from the content. If the content does not reflect the interests of the audience, the audience will go elsewhere.

To be clear about the audience's interests, publishers and editors work closely together to establish the journal's editorial objectives, explore the kinds of papers likely to meet those objectives, and create clear guidelines for potential authors. Editors brief members of the review board thoroughly on the journal's objectives. Indeed, many of the review questions set by journals for the reviewers ask the direct question: Does the paper reflect the editorial objectives of the journal?

With such clear targeting, and clear direction given to prospective authors, why, then, are up to half of all papers rejected before the review process? And why do some of those which are reviewed engender comments such as those below, given by a reviewer of a well-focused, highly academic journal:

> The topic itself is interesting but the treatment from an academic standpoint is slightly shallow … This is the kind of paper which is probably more of interest to practitioners than to academics.

Perhaps the author did not bother to investigate the journal's objectives, or perhaps the paper was rejected by the author's preferred journal and simply sent on to the next without revision. Or maybe the author just did not know how to research the targeted journal. Whatever the reason, you have no excuse now. What follows is a detailed guide on how to find the right journal and, most importantly, how to find out exactly what sort of paper the journal requires.

Let us assume first that you are starting from a position of relative ignorance. You have worked out the purpose and implication of your paper, you understand who your readers are, but now you have to find them. There are several sources of information that are set out below in what is probably the best chronological sequence for authors to adopt.

First sources of information

What you need to know is: who is reading the journal and what do they want? With all other conditions being met, targeting the right journal is the most important determinant of success. When asked why a particular paper was published in a particular journal, most editors and authors say it was because the paper was right for the journal.

When Prof. Roger Sansi-Roca won the Alfred Gell prize for 'best paper' in the *Journal of Material Culture*, he reflected that a main reason for his success was because he met the needs of the journal. His paper 'The hidden life of stones: historicity, materiality and the value of Candomblé objects in Bahia' suited the objectives of the journal, he reflected: 'In another context, it may have been poorly received, or even ignored. In academia, you always have to be very (very) aware of who is going to read your paper'.

Simple, really. Odd, when you think about it, that so many people get it wrong. Let's see how you can find out more about journals before you choose your target.

Directories

If you have no idea about any of the prospective journals that might suit your paper, you can always refer to a directory of publications. Your librarian will have at least one directory in the library. While the directory's information can be helpful, particularly for gaining a quick overview of the journal, it will only give you a superficial feel for what the journal requires. Directories are inevitably out of date. Even last year's directory won't tell you the name of a recently appointed new editor.

Respected authors

You will be familiar with the leaders in your own field and will know who is writing about topics closely linked to yours. They formed the majority of readings on the programmes and modules you have taken, and the substance of your literature review. Return to those and note where they were published.

You can find out, by carrying out a search by author, where these authors are published more widely. You can visit their university web pages and see their list of publications. You can also find out where those who cite them are being published by referring to the web pages carrying their papers. But, again, this only gives you a list of prospective journals. It doesn't give you any in-depth information about the journals or their editors.

Authorities

Find out which journals matter most to those in a position to judge you. Which journals are rated most highly by your peers? By leading academics in your department? Which journals do government assessment teams rate in determining quality? These are the people you need to impress for promotion or funding; some may even be journal reviewers. The unavoidable rule about being judged by other people is to always find out what criteria they are using. If your reference group rates one journal more highly than another, you need to know – and why.

Respected colleagues

Ask around. What do the people you most respect read? What do they have to say about the journals you have shortlisted? Where do they publish, and where did they publish first? What alternatives do they know to the journals you have selected? Is there a slightly different angle you could take to gain acceptance by a journal that may be more narrowly focused, but no less respected?

Impact factors

Some people rely on 'Impact Factors' which are calculated by measuring how often the 'average article' in any particular journal has been cited within a particular period (usually two years). It is far from a perfect way to measure the quality of a journal. For example, the 'average article' calculation does not distinguish between different types of published works, and may therefore include full-length papers, reviews, editorials and even letters. The Impact Factor can be increased by publishing more review papers, by authors citing the journal more often in their reference lists and by editors citing specific papers in their editorials. Nevertheless, it is a widely used performance measure and therefore one which most publishers keenly observe.

In-depth journal analysis

At best, your investigations using the above methods will only give you a brief overview of the journals that might be suitable and the names and addresses of editors. Unfortunately, this is where too many authors stop. That would be a little like going to a dating site and simply finding out your date's first name and telephone number. What are you going to talk about over dinner? Before you write your paper, you will need a thorough idea of the journal's requirements. Finding these out is easy but takes time

Ideally, you will already be familiar with a few journals, and one in particular may have been informing your research. Being part of that academic conversation will help you understand where to insert yourself and to what academic community you belong.

Reflecting on her long tenure as editor of the *Journal for the Scientific Study of Religion*, Marie Cornwall (2010) offers aspiring authors advice on getting published and is clear about the importance of recognizing that journals have their own niches and avoiding what she calls 'journal shopping'. A paper submitted to a journal containing no references to any previous paper in that journal is less likely to succeed, she says. One reason is that the lack of attention to that specific journal means the author has not been reading it regularly and therefore is not part of that field: 'One cannot contribute to the cumulativeness of scholarship if one lacks a sense of the field itself', she says. Further, if the paper lacks specific journal/field-related references, or dated references, how does the author claim to be contributing to that field's body of knowledge? This problem can be compounded if the author pads the paper with their own work. A technical issue is that this makes the process of carrying out 'blind review' more difficult, but it also raised the question, she says, of how much the author is paying attention to work beside their own.

To understand a journal, you must learn to read it critically, looking beyond the obvious for hints below the surface. If your library subscribes to the journal, or to the database covering the journal, you can easily access journals by volume and year. Hard copies are less likely to be available in your own library if you want to browse them in person, but the librarian may be able to obtain them through interlibrary loans. Most publishers will respond to a direct request for a sample copy of the journal, either digitally or in print. In either case, having your own copy is convenient and allows you to make notes against published articles. You should do this in addition to reading several issues thoroughly. You may be tempted to look at just one issue, but without doubt you should read several issues – three is probably a minimum. After all, your objective is to become familiar with the journal, not just to know how to spell its name. But which three issues in any one volume should you choose?

The first and last issues in any one volume (year) are those which will probably contain the most clues about the journal, its future, and editorial preferences; it is in these issues that strategically minded editors discuss their objectives, problems and aspirations. In the volume's first issue editors, who will usually have several months' or even a year's worth of papers held in advance, will often describe what themes are to come. As they anticipate the new year, they will also often comment on the kinds of papers they hope to receive, or the improvements they will be making to the journal. In the final issue of the volume, editors will often summarize the year's contributions and comment on what they consider to be the high and low points.

Reading the editor's own published articles will give you information about his or her background, speciality and needs. Many editors are well published; finding their articles will not be difficult. What do they say about the field in which you are both working? What work has the editor done which impacts on your own? The objective here is not to be sycophantic: you are not trying to become a clone of an editor and nor are you seeking to fall into the trap of becoming afraid to challenge existing theory particularly when that theory may be the editor's. Good editors warm to a fair challenge. What is important is the knowledge base upon which you are building.

Notes to authors

All journals publish Notes for prospective authors. Most carry them on their web pages prominently, but if they do not there will be a reference to them and where they can be found. The Notes vary in detail from general to specific. At the very least, and of most importance to any prospective author, they should include the editorial objectives. The examples below illustrate how clearly some top-class journals state their objectives; on its website[1], The *Australian Journal of Botany* states its aims clearly:

> The *Australian Journal of Botany* is an international journal for publication of original research in plant science. The journal publishes in the areas of ecology and ecophysiology; invasive biology; conservation

biology and biodiversity; forest biology and management; cell and molecular biology; palaeobotany and biogeography; reproductive biology and genetics; mycology and pathology; structure and development; and aquatic botany.

(CSIRO Publishing n.d.)

There are easily identifiable links leading to its publishing policy, scope and detailed guidelines for authors. Further, as with most journal sites, prospective authors can read a selection of past papers, including those that have been most cited. This will give you excellent, inside-information about the kinds of papers likely to be accepted.

The *China Journal of Accounting Research*[2] is clear on its website about the type of paper that would be suitable, not only in its content, but also its theoretical frameworks:

> The focus of the *China Journal of Accounting Research* is to publish theoretical and empirical research papers that use contemporary research methodologies to investigate issues about accounting, corporate finance, auditing and corporate governance in the Greater China region, countries related to the Belt and Road Initiative, and other emerging and developed markets. The Journal encourages the applications of economic and sociological theories to analyze and explain accounting issues within the legal and institutional framework, and to explore accounting issues under different capital markets accurately and succinctly.
>
> (Elsevier n.d.)

The journal *Sociology*[3] describes itself as the 'flagship journal of the British Sociological Association' (The British Sociological Association n.d.). It explains that it 'publishes peer-reviewed articles advancing theoretical understanding and reporting empirical research about the widest range of sociological topics. *Sociology* encourages submissions using quantitative and qualitative research methods'.

The website information also describes the journal's activities as including full-length papers, shorter notes, comments, and reviews. The latter possibilities open up more opportunities for potential authors.

The above examples are good illustrations of clear and pointed Notes to Authors. They leave no doubt as to the direction of the journals described, and therefore leave the contributor no excuse for submitting anything less than appropriate, nor any reason why the editor or reviewers should tolerate anything less.

The Notes in most journals continue beyond editorial objectives to specify how authors should present papers. This is known in the industry as the journal's 'house style'. It is a sure give-away that authors have not researched the journal when they submit papers in a completely different format than that required. Many journal editors become quickly impatient with such submissions, suspecting, probably rightly, that the author has been sending the same paper to other journals as well. Do not be surprised if, having failed to pay attention to the specific journal's specification, your paper is immediately returned to you. The editors of the *Journal of East African Natural History* (Nature Kenya/East African Natural History Society 2022) for example, are clear about consequences:

> Contributors are encouraged to study the most recent version of the Instructions to Authors which can be found on www.bioone.org. Papers that do not conform to the above guidelines will be returned to the author for correction before review.

I will discuss the presentation in more detail later; the objectives here are to make sure that you target the right journal and begin to plan the paper in accordance with that journal's objectives and requirements.

Objective criteria

If the Notes to Authors do not tell you enough about what the journal is looking for, write to the editor and ask for a statement of criteria. You need to know how editors and reviewers make their decisions. What exactly do they look for? Many journals have a *pro forma* which guides their reviewers. Write to the editor of your chosen journal and ask for one. I review in more detail how to understand editors and reviewers in the next chapter.

People who read and influence the journal are very clear about the criteria. When, in my earlier research, I asked people to rank and weight journals, the results were consistent per journal. It was not difficult to analyze the results and get a clear profile. This means that readers, editors and reviewers of well-focused journals know what the journal stands for. It is only one step further to ask the readers, editors and reviewers to articulate their understanding and convert the results into practical guidelines for authors. As this becomes easier, with good data management, it will increasingly become the norm.

As a prospective author for a selected journal, you not only have the right but even the responsibility to demand clear statements of quality criteria from the editor and publisher. A journal that cannot articulate this, and is unwilling to share it, is a journal with a questionable presence or future, and may one of those known as 'predatory'. For better or for worse, academics are being judged against clear and measurable criteria in many parts of their work: the journal papers they write are no exception.

The Research Excellence Framework (REF) in the UK, for example, publishes the criteria it uses to assess research outputs and to award its stars, ranging from top quality (4*) to minimal (1*) and then, worst of all, to 'unclassified'. Their definition of excellence stresses research that is 'world-leading', original, rigorous and significant. The coveted star ratings are awarded according to the degree with which research meets those standards. Interestingly, the 'unclassified' category refers to research that does not meet national standards. Those standards may seem elusive, mysterious or unattainable, but less so the more you read papers from your prospective journal and become more familiar with the high, accepted standards you find there.

Clues from papers

The published papers themselves will give you further insight. Make a habit of deconstructing them against quality criteria. Authors who consistently contribute to the same journals will frequently refer to papers previously published in the journal. You can do an online search restricting the areas to keyword for subject and journal. This will give you a list of papers published in your area in the journals you are targeting. You can then create a map showing how the journal has traced the development of your topic, and what previously published authors have said and how.

Building on the body of knowledge therefore becomes a more careful exercise, given that your targeted journals are those you have decided are the best places to publish your material. Working from that assumption, it is only reasonable to cite their contributions to the body of knowledge.

Widening the field

Suppose you are not starting from scratch? What if you are absolutely convinced that there is only one journal worth writing for? Think again. Ask yourself why you are concentrating exclusively on one outlet. There may be other good journals that may not be as widely known as your selected journal, but which are respected within their area.

One of the more serious pitfalls awaiting authors is their conviction that they know a journal well simply because they have heard a great deal about it or have seen it referenced frequently. That journal may therefore be popular, and for many good reasons, but it is not necessarily the only one available, or the right one for you. It is still wise to go through the exercises described above, even if you believe you will commit yourself to one journal. Test your up-to-date knowledge about the journal by reading it and contacting the editor and publisher as discussed above. Do not allow yourself to be blinkered by your own convictions, particularly if you have little empirical proof for your conclusions.

During the course of my earlier research into journal publishing practice, we asked published authors to name the chief competitors of the journals we were researching. That question generated between three and 12 responses, with an average of four competitors per journal. These were journals that, in the authors' opinions, were alternative sources of publication. As an exercise, list as many complementary journals as you can for the journal you are now targeting. If you find this exercise difficult, it may be time to get to know the full range of journals available to you.

Publishers often give talks to prospective authors about getting published. They list most of the points already covered here (Feinstein and Hobbs 2008) and emphasize that one of the most important choices an author can make is to select the right journal. They also suggest authors ask:

- What is the readership and usage?
- Is it international?
- Is it peer-reviewed: how long will this take?
- Who is the editor?
- Who is on the editorial board?
- Who publishes in the journal?
- Is it on the Institute of Scientific Information (ISI) Citation Database?
- Available online and printed?
- Is it published by a major publisher or association?

Trying it on

Now that you have a shortlist of potential journals and are well acquainted with what they publish and how, you may decide to approach the editor with your idea. Many journals actively encourage this for specific sections because they may be asking for something slightly different than that found in the main body of the journal. If there is a 'news' section, for example, they may be targeting the non-specialist reader and may accept shorter pieces such as conference reports or bulletins about works in progress, emerging advances or even opinion pieces.

But what about sending the main editor a synopsis of your full article? Editors' propensities to welcome initial enquiries vary from journal to journal. Some expect authors to be familiar with the journal and its requirements, making the synopsis stage not only unnecessary but tedious. Their view is that if the author knows what to do and how to do it, why do they not just get on with it? Why waste the editor's time in the interim, reading a lengthy and sometimes boring abstract? These editors only make their judgements based on the finished article. There are, however, other editors who appreciate an author first testing the idea. This would be more likely in a fast-moving field where the journal rapidly publishes papers before they go out of date. An editor of that kind of journal may already have an article or two poised for publication that covers exactly the same material you may have in mind. If you do decide to send an abstract first, make sure you do it properly. It would be a shame for your potentially good article never to get published merely because you described it poorly. More guidance is given later in this book.

Now, we will explore how to find the ideal funder for your project.

Funders do not want to fund your research

At a forum to discuss European Union research funding, delegates were shocked to be greeted by the opening statement: 'We are not interested in funding your research'. In other words, the EU does not seek partnerships with people who only want to fund their own pet interest or academic speciality.

That show-stopping statement applies to all funders: they are not interested in individual research projects, or sponsoring conferences or books. It is not the research they are funding, but the outcome. However well-intended and important some projects may be, asking a funder for money will be futile. Fortunately for the researcher prepared to research the funding options, funders are eager to save your time. Their guidance notes are clear.

Potential funders need to be able to see, quickly and clearly, that yours is a partnership that can work. You must be clear about what the issues are. These are too easily taken for granted. It is important to take a step back and look at the funder's most basic critical issues.

Janet Lewis, former Research Director of the Joseph Rowntree Foundation, described her experience of research proposals which do not clearly state what they are about:

> There's the focus of the issue – does it fit into the priorities that we've identified? Have they addressed the issues? ... the other thing is how

people are proposing to do the work, and even though I think proposals have got better over the last few years, we still get an awful lot that are under specified in terms of the method.

Those reasons affect applicants' success more than any other I discovered. Firstly, and most importantly, the researcher fails to articulate the issue. The reviewer finds it hard to get a clear picture as to what it is about or why it is important. Poor articulation of a problem or issue will often indicate to a funder a lack of organizational or communication ability, both of which are vital to successfully concluded research projects.

Secondly, the reviewer may know what the proposal is about, but the proposal does not fit funding priorities. The research proposal may be expertly written, the question well-framed, and the method exquisitely designed. The outcomes may be clear, the timescales and budget accurate and the references of researcher and research team impeccable. If the proposal does not, however, fit with the priorities and ethos of the funder in question, it will fail.

It may help to examine here one specific example. I will focus on 'abrdn, the Financial Fairness Trust'. Their website[4] describes them as an independent charitable foundation, aiming to 'contribute towards strategic change which improves financial well-being in the UK. We want everyone to have a decent standard of living and have more control over their finances'.

There is, of course, a page with links directly to funding information, but in the interest of reducing failure rates and time wasted, it is wise to first read the background. The Trust funds 15–20 grants each year, with each ranging between £10,000 and £200,000, to researchers from charities, bodies and universities.

Prospective researchers can then click on links to read about the Trust's funding guidelines, their helpful information about creating a budget, or they could, ill-advisedly, go straight to download the application form.

The research guidelines notes are clear. These begin with a few pages of information about the Trust, including its history and ethos. A useful section contains information about their beneficiaries – an important aspect that can also be seen on most other funders' websites. It helps to read this to be able to gauge how your research, and the Trust's beneficiaries, may align. There is also specific information about three key areas of their focus: income, spending and assets. Detail is then provided about who they fund, where they fund and how they fund.

A separate section lists the six criteria against which they assess proposals. These are so specific it would seem any prospective applicant should structure their proposal around them, such as demonstrating exactly how the proposal fits the programme and matches the Trust's strategy. Applicants should also spend time describing 'delivery', both by saying how they are sufficiently competent to deliver what they propose, and also how they will disseminate their findings. The importance of understanding the funding context is particularly obvious here:

> Applications for work where we have already provided significant funds will be a lower priority. We are also mindful of the work of other funders and will give a lower priority to areas where there is already substantial funding in comparison to other issues.

Ideally, prospective applicants will read all this information and ensure they are not on the list of the 13 examples of what the Trust does not fund. Once applications are made, there is a shortlisting process, and the site kindly informs prospective applicants that 'Unfortunately, we have to make difficult choices and therefore have to reject a number of good applications. Just because you're not shortlisted does not necessarily mean that we do not think you are doing good and valuable work'. And yet, some people apply who have not met even the basic requirements. Like most funders, the first stage in the decision-making process is when staff sift through applications, eliminating those that are obviously unsuitable and will not be referred onto the Research Grants Committee. The most common reason for instant rejection is that the proposal does not meet the aims of the Trust.

Think about that! Read the sentence again, and ask yourself: how could the proposal *not* meet the aims of the Trust? What were applicants thinking? Evidently, they were not thinking about what makes a good proposal, the most important criterion of which will be a match between funder and applicant.

Similar principles apply to government funders. The largest funders in most countries are governments, spending taxpayers' money on research that needs to show a return on that investment. That return does not need to be expressed in financial terms, but the government must be able to see what will happen as a result of its spending. Some researchers are suspicious that government funders are skewing their research priorities to match selected topics decreed by the government. In the UK, for example, this is unlikely due to what is known as the 'Haldane Principal'. This principle is designed to protect the independence of government-funded research councils. The principle takes its name from Richard Burdon Haldane, Viscount Haldane of Cloan (1856–1928) described by the Dictionary of National Biography as a Scottish statesman, lawyer and philosopher. Politically, his sympathies were left of centre, first as a liberal MP for East Lothian for 26 years and then as a Labour peer in opposition in the House of Lords. But it was his eye for organization which most influenced British government in the early 20th century. As Secretary of State for War between 1905 and 1912, he reorganized the army; in 1917 he chaired a committee to reorganize the government itself, which he found had suffered from haphazard growth.

Most significantly for those in education, Haldane was an early and vigorous champion of increased educational opportunities for people of all backgrounds and dedicated much of his career to helping 'new' or what he called 'civic' universities develop in and outside London. He was one of the founders of the London School of Economics, a council member of University College, London, president of Birkbeck College, Fellow and council member of the British Academy and eventually Chancellor of the University of Bristol from 1917 until his death in 1928.

In 1904 he chaired the government committee which recommended creating the Universities Grant Committee to advise the government on how to allocate funds. In 1909 he chaired a Royal Commissions on university education which reported in 1918. It was then that what we now call the 'Haldane Principle' emerged, namely, that research money derived from government sources would not be linked to government agendas.

The Quinquennial Review of the Research Councils (2001) reaffirmed the primacy of this principle, noting that successive governments have all endorsed the Haldane Principle as one of the prime protectors of the scientific integrity of research. The 2017 UK Higher Education and Research Act also reaffirmed it (Higher Education and Research Act 2017).

Tied to independence accountability is transparency, particularly in regard to the funder's obligation to report on its activities, whether to government or to the Charity Commission, for example. While on the one hand the government has no right to dictate what research is to be carried out using government money, it has the right and the obligation to see that public money is appropriately spent. This means that research councils must unfailingly report on how and why funds are allocated and demonstrate in sometimes painstaking detail that it is responsibly doing so. As long as this occurs, the Haldane Principle will no doubt maintain its influence, and researchers will enjoy a friendly distance from government. But it is also reasonable to expect that if successive generations of researchers and research councils fail to respect the obligation of public accountability, a less tolerant government may question the ethics of arms-length research which wastes precious resources.

Understanding this may provide insight for researchers who seek to form partnerships with those who receive government money. It can, perhaps, remove some of the frustration many people express about the detail, bureaucracy and seemingly onerous reporting and accountability methods used by the public sector.

Talk to them!

If you are uncertain about any aspect of the proposal, or whether the funder is right for you, just ask. One funder expressed frustration that prospective researchers fail to understand what the funder stands for:

> Sometimes I can't understand why they brought this to us because it's so obvious that they've not thought that one through. You have to think sometimes that people are sitting in their garret alone somewhere, writing, and that's not the way to develop a really good research proposal.

Talking to them is often the best way to ensure you are heading for a mutually satisfactory relationship, and this is something applicants often overlook, according to another funder: 'They can ring up anytime during the tender process', she stresses. This reflects the aims of the organization itself, which is committed to transparency, she explains: 'We're not just transparent in terms of product but of process'.

For proposals that involve an iterative process, where the funder gives feedback on more than one version, the conversations may allow an applicant to deviate slightly from a standard specification by adding a note that more detail in one area needs to be explored. One funder advises people to:

> Put in a statement that x, y, or z can be met as expected, but request a meeting to discuss further. This shows respect, shows that you're listening. That's the added value, this shows how we could benefit further. It pushes the boundaries.

In another example, the successful applicant told me that they were awarded a contract mainly because they had offered to meet and discuss issues with the funder. They said:

> The [government] department sent a request for some information in a particular area. I think there were about 15 key academics who they identified. When I asked them why did I get the contract they said, well, out of the 15 e-mails we sent, 14 of them said – go and buy my book,

go and read my paper, except your e-mail which said – come down and let's sit and talk about the issues. So, they came sat, talked, and were impressed and the project itself then unfolded.

There is a view that if we just get on with the job and do our best we will get ahead. Unfortunately, that is wrong. When we explore who gets ahead quickly and who gets their projects approved, we find it is often the person with the deepest insider knowledge and who uses that knowledge to enrich their proposal.

Summary: choosing the right journal or funder

We have explored thus far in this chapter how important it is to target the correct journal or funder. By now, you have now done the hardest part of the work:

- Researching your audience.
- Targeting your journal or funder.
- Understanding what they expect.
- Planning how to meet those expectations.

In the next chapter I will look in more detail at the people, and the processes, that constitute journals and funding bodies.

Action points

Now it's time to start some research. Select from your library, or by some other means, between two and four 'target' journals or information about key funders. Go through the Notes for Authors/Applicants and make notes. What are their objectives? What is the scope? What are their criteria for eligibility?

Next, examine the journal's contents or funder's website. Read some articles or summaries of who they have funded. Read the editorials or funder history. Note the names on the advisory board and review board, if listed. Is anyone there whose work you know? Can you find out more?

Now you have a relationship in preparation. All you have to do is deliver the goods…

Notes

1 www.publish.csiro.au/bt/aboutthejournal.

2 www.journals.elsevier.com/china-journal-of-accounting-research.
3 www.britsoc.co.uk/publications/sociology-journal/.
4 www.financialfairness.org.uk.

References

Cornwall, Marie (2010). 'From the editor: Ten most likely ways an article submission fails to live up to publishing standard', *Journal for the Scientific Study of Religion*, 49(4): i–v.

CSIRO Publishing (n.d.). *The Australian Journal of Botany.* Available at: www.publish.csiro.au/bt/aboutthejournal

Elsevier (n.d.). *Journal Acceptance Rates: Everything You Need to Know.* Available at: https://scientific-publishing.webshop.elsevier.com/publication-process/journal-acceptance-rates/

Elsevier (n.d.). *The China Journal of Accounting Research.* Available at: www.journals.elsevier.com/china-journal-of-accounting-research

Feinstein, Jessica and Graham Hobbs (2008). 'Writing a journal article: Guidance for authors', *Editors' Bulletin*, 4(3): 96–99.

Higher Education and Research Act (2017). Available at: https://www.legislation.gov.uk/ukpga/2017/29/section/103/enacted

Nature Kenya/East African Natural History Society (2022). *Journal of East African Natural History*, 111. Available at: https://bioone.org/journals/journal-of-east-african-natural-history

The British Sociological Association (n.d.). *The Journal Sociology.* Available at: www.britsoc.co.uk/publications/sociology-journal/

9 UNDERSTANDING EDITORS, REVIEWERS, READERS

Introduction

If you were asked to sit down right now and write a letter, you would surely ask three obvious questions: to whom, about what, and why? We are all pestered almost daily with unsolicited communications from people wanting us to buy a new product or, at the very least, enter our name to win a massive prize for which we have supposedly been shortlisted. Most people don't like those kinds of communications and refer to them as junk mail.

But suppose you received a message from your local supermarket, thanking you for using their loyalty card and informing you that the next time you do your shopping you will receive two free bottles of the wine you usually buy and a free, matching artisan cheese board. Would you accept that offer? Very likely. That is the difference between junk mail and well-targeted mail. One is a blanket communication paying no respect to the person receiving it and the other is created with the person's own preferences and habits in mind. We have all experienced both kinds of communication and know to which we respond the best.

Why is it then that so many authors send editors and funders junk mail? As we investigated thoroughly in Chapter 8, editors reject immediately up to half the papers they receive simply because they are not suited to that particular journal's brief. Editors are inundated with inappropriate papers on subjects outside the scope of the journal, or papers written in a style clearly unsuitable for that journal's audience. The first wave of scrutiny in a funders' office does the same. On the latter point, that is why during the last decade or so universities have moved to insist that any funding application is subjected first to internal scrutiny. Before bemoaning what may seem like an unnecessary and unwelcome extra level of bureaucracy, spare a thought for the weary funder who is tired of receiving ill-prepared and inconsiderately targeted junk mail. The problem is not simply on an individual level – the funder must evaluate even the most unlikely applications, taking time and money away from more worthy projects.

DOI: 10.4324/9781003259718-11

Whenever you are writing for publication or creating a funding proposal, you are trying to convey your ideas and evidence to another person. As with most publishing and funding bodies, scholarly endeavours rely on several layers of people to help your work reach the final reader in the best shape possible. Each layer is populated with individuals who have slightly different needs and standards. You need to satisfy them all.

Your link in the chain

I will begin here with journals. As described in the previous chapters, authors are involved in a publishing process composed of several different people seeking different benefits. Think of the publishing process as a supply chain. At the head of the chain is the manufacturer, the person who makes the product. In this case, the product is a paper destined for an academic journal, and the manufacturer is you.

You could simply photocopy your paper and send it to your friends, but this is insufficient to help you reach a wider, unfamiliar, audience or guarantee the level of credibility and quality demanded by your discipline. Fortunately, there are distributors whose job is to quality test your paper and link it to a journal with other papers, let people know it is available, deliver it to those who have ordered it, and collect money to pay for all their activities. The distributor, in this sense, is the publisher.

That could be the end of the story, but a few questions arise. How will the distributor decide what papers to publish? How will the distributor keep up with the changing state-of-the-art? The distributor appoints an expert to read the papers first and select those which deserve publication. This person is usually called an editor.

This, again, could be the end of the story and often is for the less academic and more practice-based journals. But now much more is hanging in the balance. Institutions are rating academics on their publication records, and the institutions themselves are being rated by others. Someone has to be sure that the best decisions are being made. What if the single editor does not know everything about every variation in the field? What if their best friend, or arch-rival, is the author? How will the distributor and the editor know that decisions are being made fairly and by the most informed minds? They appoint a team to help the editor called the 'review board'. Normally, publication in a reviewed (or refereed – the terms are used synonymously) journal counts for more than publication in an unreviewed, or editor-only reviewed journal, magazine, or book.

Now, between the manufacturer and final publication, we already have three links in the chain: publisher, editor, and review board. But, as with most learned journals, readers usually gain access through a library. The librarian is therefore another intermediary between manufacturer and reader, making four links. The librarian may be informed by another intermediary known as an agent who will often handle all the billing requirements. As the paper will be distributed electronically, we can expand 'library' to include Internet. Finally, the reader will have the paper available to read.

Each person involved in the chain has compatible, but slightly different, needs and pressures. Each will approach the paper and individual journal with slightly different questions.

> Author: 'Can I get my paper accepted in this journal?'
> Editor: 'Does it meet the aims of the journal and its audience?'
> Review board: 'Is it the right quality?'
> Publisher: 'Is the journal performing to market expectations?'
> Librarian: 'How can I give access to it?'
> Reader: 'Where can I read it? Is it useful to me?'

The supply chain remains much the same for digital communication. Whether the final output is paper-based or electronic, it must still be distributed around a network, it must still be reviewed if it is to count towards a publication record, and it must still be accessible to the reader. Authors can always go direct to reader, through the post or through a blog. But that, alone, will not presume quality control, and it is the presumption of quality control which makes a refereed journal and the papers within it significant.

Each member of this supply chain has a need to fulfil. If each member of the chain understands the others' needs, they are more likely to be able to satisfy them. Once each member has done that once, and learned what they need, they can then move towards building a relationship with the other members of the chain. As an author, you might find you can publish regularly in the same journal or even another journal published by the same distributor. This brings you to the ultimate goal: how to repeat the performance, and possibly, if desired, move towards reviewing and editing yourself. I review those choices in more detail in Chapter 12. And, if that seems too ambitious, remember that we are all part of the same community, although we play different parts in the whole. Academic publishers, editors, and reviewers are not strangers, they are people like you, people like your colleagues, your supervisor. Indeed, it is likely they are your colleagues.

I will now turn to investigate these people, what they need, and how you can make their job easier.

Understanding editors

Editors are busy people – always and by definition. No publisher will appoint an editor who is out of touch with the field or has no reputation amongst their peers. Editing a journal will, during an average year, involve hundreds of extra hours of work. Included in the editor's remit is: advising the publisher on the direction of the journal; agreeing editorial strategy; advising on a review board; monitoring the workings of the review board to ensure quality and timeliness; accepting papers for the review process; corresponding with reviewers; taking their feedback and passing it on to the author; seeing the paper through one or several revisions; making sure all the documentation is in order; selecting which issue the paper should appear in based on pagination requirements and editorial balance; sending it to the publisher in time for the agreed production schedule; looking over the proofs; answering queries from sub-editors; and finally sending the approved version back to the publisher on schedule. The last thing they need is junk mail.

Editors are respected within their institutions and their academic community. They are not, typically, has-beens who retire to the south of France with only a few journal papers to look over before lunch. Publishers are not interested in people who have left the network. Editors are extremely active, time-pressured people constantly involved in teaching, researching, writing, and editing.

Any academic, and even some students, appreciate that an academic's life is not always an easy one. There are classes to teach, papers to mark, students to supervise, committees to appear on, conferences to attend, papers to write... and then on top of that load the editor will elect to take responsibility for a journal. Spare a few moments to consider exactly what that task entails.

For an editor, some authors are good news and some not so good. Some make their lives easier, and some make them wonder if they should give up editing and let someone else have all the headaches. The best are welcomed not only because their worthwhile papers improve the journal, and therefore the editor's stature but because their professionalism smooths the flow.

Perhaps the biggest misconception about journal editors is that they are in it for the money. The reality is far from that: they will receive a modest stipend, perhaps of £500 per issue, and often an amount they can use to pay for administrative help. Converting those numbers to an hourly wage would put them far before the minimum. Therefore, one may ask why they do it.

Editors are more than faceless academics – they are real people with busier lives than most people. The amount of time they invest in journal editing is not only financially unrewarding, but it is often on top of everything else that they already do in the course of their careers. What is it, then, that motivates an editor to take on all this work?

An act of citizenship: I interviewed Prof. Rhys Williams on what it was like to edit two journals: *Social Problems* and the *Journal for the Scientific Study of Religion*. In describing the role of an editor, he began by saying: 'most of journal editing is an act of citizenship'.

Many editors agree that the status of being an editor is not to be under-estimated, particularly if the journal is the official journal of a professional association with which one is involved. Being held in esteem by one's colleagues is important to any academic. It leads to recognition at professional meetings where people will want to seek you out, meet you, and confer about topics that go beyond the journal itself. Prof. Williams suggests that being an editor, therefore, confers a sense of 'having arrived' as a professional, where 'being chosen is a type of validation of one's academic record and reputation'.

Peer recognition is important, other editors agreed when I interviewed them, adding comments like 'there is some status in being a member of a Board and a team' with, others said, the opportunity to help shape a Journal's policies and practices.

Another editor commented that if the journal is well regarded by the people it is aimed at, then:

> one can feel a great sense of satisfaction that one is doing an important job in a way that one's peers approve of … it is a positively recognised form of scholarly endeavour, and helps very much in terms of developing one's academic career.

Shaping the discipline is an ideal which is often expressed by editors. By helping authors 'shape' their papers, editors can in turn influence the journal and the field as a whole. Prof. Joseph Smith, when he was editor of History, summarized the kinds of impacts an editor may have:

> The job of editor is demanding but also personally satisfying because it leads to the publication of a high quality scholarly journal which promotes the aim of the [History Association] to be the 'voice of history'; gives a wide range of historians (and not just those in academic posts) the opportunity to develop and publish their work and contribute to the historical debate on their particular topic; on a more parochial level having '*History*' enhances the reputation of the History department at my university.

These are the sorts of thoughts expressed by others who often said that their greatest sense of satisfaction as an editor came when they saw a paper they had helped 'shape' eventually reach publication. One editor described the idea of 'shaping' by saying that their overwhelming motive was a desire to shape the discipline, through shaping the papers that get published. This suggests that the first dimension of shaping is upholding and enforcing standards of quality: 'All editors want whatever articles appear under their editorship to be of the highest quality they can reasonably be – to bolster the reputation of the subdiscipline, the journal, and their stewardship'.

Editors consider the effort of influencing the field through journal editing as a significant contribution to the academic field one operates within, either a more specialist field or the discipline as a whole. This is often described as a scholarly service to both authors and readers, and also as a privilege. As one editor put it, 'Editing a journal is also a way in which to influence the evolution of one's field, possibly for many years to come, so it brings with it a sense of accomplishment if you do that in a responsible way'.

Another reason is that the role demands they read hundreds of papers each year, thus keeping on top – and even ahead – of all important developments in the field.

Staying in front: Editing journals is an opportunity to read research at the cutting edge. Being the first person to look at a paper sent to one of the world's most respected journals gives an editor a privileged position of insight. Keeping ahead of the game is an important benefit of being an editor. Being an editor keeps them in touch with developments in their fields, both because they read often ground-breaking papers, but also because new books that are published in their area are sent to the editorial office for review.

The above comments shed some useful light on the role of an editor, and perhaps will inspire you to work even more sympathetically with these people who give up so much time to benefit the discipline. It might even lead you to think about becoming an editor someday. After all, they are just people like you. The image of the unfriendly critic waiting to humiliate you through rejection – one of the fears we discussed earlier which often prevents people from publishing – is simply not true.

To understand more about an editor, use the same technique as described earlier – read the journal! Read the editorials. What does the editor say about the current issue of the journal? Note comments like 'Helen Brown's paper on the use of slang in Puerto Rico is a good example of the literature tested in practice'. That is a fairly clear statement of what the editor likes to see in a paper. Other editorials might centre on topical issues that capture the editor's attention; conversely, some may indicate topics or treatments of topics that the editor finds overworked. A month after an editor has sworn never to publish yet another treatise on 'the crisis of masculinity' is not the time to send them your brilliant summary of it. Again, editorial preference is likely to be more clearly stated in the first and last issues of a volume. Not only will observing editors' comments help you judge how best to approach your paper but referring to them in any correspondence will impress the editor that you are taking your job seriously and, at the very least, improve the chances of starting discussions.

Not all journals welcome preliminary letters (and their Notes for Contributors will tell you about this). For those that do, submitting an abstract of your paper accompanied by a letter which begins 'Your observation in Vol. 12 No. 6 that little work has been done to research the effects of carbon monoxide on pond flora helped me direct the paper that I am now preparing' is quite impressive.

Editors will often, in their editorials, comment on a paper that has made a particular impact and discuss the reasons why. Many journals give annual prizes for the 'best papers' and the editor is likely to say why certain papers were judged as best.

When the editorial direction of a journal changes, this too may be commented on in an editorial. A change in direction often accompanies a change in editor. Discussion of the new editor's ambitions will offer further insight into the future of the journal and the papers being sought.

I will now take a look at other members of the team and consider how you can get to know them and perhaps get involved.

Understanding reviewers

Because editors' names, and sometimes faces, are publicly connected with journals we are more likely to picture them as real people. Reviewers, however, are expected to remain anonymous. Who are these mysterious arbiters of quality? They are people like you, people you know, professors at your own university, someone you saw present a paper at a conference. Nobody mysterious, nobody forbidding. After all, the proper term for the process is 'peer review'. A peer is someone who is your equal. Having said that, they have worked hard to build a reputation for excellent work and scholarship, which is why they are asked to review papers. Membership of a review board is by invitation, which means that the general criterion is a person's scholarship and reputation in the field.

The benefits reviewers derive from their work are similar to the benefits experienced by editors. They keep up to date in their own fields, they keep in touch with who is writing interesting papers based on original thought or research and they improve their own reputation by being associated with a good-quality journal. That does not mean it is an easy or lucrative job – they do not receive sufficient remuneration or tangible benefits.

Although in a blind review process the reviewer supposedly does not know the author and vice versa, we have to remember that it is a small world. Particularly if you write about a highly specialized topic, it is likely that only a handful of people would be competent enough to comment on it. Who are they? Do you know what they have written? Do you know their particular sensitivities? How does their work fit with yours? Could you work with them? Could you become one?

Many journals operate a dynamic and organic approach to reviewing, where an author who has published with them is sent a paper similar to the author's own work, method or milieu and asked to review it. You will be given appropriate guidance on the criteria, and your review will be read along with, usually, two or three others.

Other journals may operate with review boards where only the members of the review boards will referee papers. Yet, many of those journals also use non-members for papers which fall outside the normal remit, or when existing reviewers are over-loaded with work. Some journals have 'associate' boards specifically designed for new or less experienced reviewers to become involved with the process, and formal training courses are sometimes given.

Reviewers might read anything from one or two papers a year to several papers each month. They read each carefully and in great detail so that they can send constructive comments back. Some journals supply reviewers with a form to draw their attention to the specific quality criteria being sought and to help the reviewer respond in a methodical fashion. The review process is normally a 'blind' one, which means that the editor knows who the author is and to which reviewers he or she is sending the paper, but authors don't know who is reviewing it. Reviewers do not know who the author is because the editor has removed the author's name and affiliation from the front of the paper. Why? Just to make sure that everyone is playing fair, that the reviewer is not easing the path of someone because he or she knows them, and that he or she is not overawed by someone with a towering reputation in their field. Editors will normally send a paper to at least two and often three reviewers and may collate their comments before giving feedback to the author.

Editors will normally send a reviewer papers that reflect that individual reviewer's own subject knowledge, expertise and interest. The author can therefore assume that the paper is being read by someone who is not only a recognized leader in the field, but someone who reads papers similar to the author's regularly and thoroughly. They can also assume that they do not have two heads, green fangs or put their socks on much differently to anyone else. They are people like us: in fact, they are 'us' – teachers, researchers, authors. What can you expect to hear from them? How are they likely to give their comments? In words like these:

> To increase the value of the paper, I recommend that the authors go back a step or two to show how the attributes are selected, rated and then analysed – the subject matter is very interesting and the cited examples are very relevant.

Now, that's not so bad. There is something you can work with, delivered in a tone which does not send you scurrying away, deflated, and demoralized. That is what you should, and can, expect from the better journals. Unfortunately, not all reviewers provide feedback in such constructive tones. Normally, the better editors do not approve of callous criticism any more than authors do and diplomatically filter out terse review comments.

Reviewers will each have a slightly different perspective on what is important in the subject area and will themselves be at different stages in their thinking. No one claims that reviewers are perfect or even unanimous. An editor is not seeking total uniformity of opinion, and neither should the author. Each reviewer's feedback will give something new to ponder. Only when they are completely opposed to the prospective paper on every criteria may the editor seek a new opinion or override with their own judgement.

That quality of exclusivity, the 'old-boy network', has long been a weakness of the review process and people are right to criticize it. Some review committees do not operate on a 'blind' basis, and others are increasing moving to this option. We will review in Chapter 12 how you can become involved as a reviewer.

Time out: inside the true life of reviewers

Whether for a journal or a funding proposal, reviewers share the same context. They may even be the same person. So, exactly who are they and how will they be engaging with your paper or your proposal? There is a tendency amongst inexperienced academics to talk about 'the journal' or 'the funder'. Both these are entities populated by people. Your first engagement with any of them will be with a staff member employed by the journal or the funder. If you are skilled enough to have crafted your paper or proposal to meet the main criteria of the journal or funder, your work will be passed into the review system. That means, handed over to a reviewer.

The reviewers, for journals and funders, are not employed by the funder or the funding organization. They are academics employed by a university. Their main job is to teach, research, write and perform almost countless, and increasing, administrative tasks. In addition to that, they have agreed with a journal or funder that they are available to review papers and proposals. Their name and expertise are now part of the publisher's or funder's database. They will have ticked several boxes to enable a close match between their experience and any potential paper or proposal. These are likely to include, minimally, a discipline, sub-discipline, geographic region, and method. If you are proposing, for example, a research project involving large-scale sur-veys to test a given hypothesis about young people's changing use of social media in South-East Asia, that proposal is likely to be sent to Dr/Prof. Blogs who is an expert in quantitative research, has focused mainly on young peo-ple, written widely about social media, and has done most of their fieldwork in South-East Asia. It will not be sent to me, an expert in qualitative research focusing on generational value change in the UK. Further, if by chance it is sent to me, the email will ask me to review first the summary to ensure it meets my expertise and interest and that I have no conflict of interest (by, for example, being the supervisor of the author or funding applicant). It will also ask me to commit to a deadline, usually two to four weeks hence. In this case, I would decline to review as I do not have the training or competence to review quantitative work in detail. On the same day that I receive that email from the publisher or funder, so do several other potential reviewers. Each paper or proposal will have two or three reviewers who independently assess the paper or proposal.

The above section may give the impression that reviewers are all highly organized, efficient people able to take cool, calculating views based on years of experience and knowledge. And that's true. But consider now what ac-tually happens when they get around to reading your paper or proposal. Inevitably, reviewers are busy people, and they need to fit time to read your paper or proposal into an already packed schedule. Imagine you are them: It is three o'clock one afternoon when you settle down in your office to give the submission your undivided attention. At least, that's the plan. Suddenly, there is a knock on the door, and it is a colleague wanting to know if you have received the invitation to their book launch. You chat for a moment, wish them well and return to your desk. Now, where were you? It seems like an interesting proposal, but you have not quite understood its purpose, and you are already three pages in. Maybe, you think, you will feel better after a break, so you pack up, head home and on the way realize you have not, as planned, picked up the pasta for dinner. Stop at the supermarket, do some shopping and get home half an hour late. The kids are hungry, but excited about their sports day and you all chat while you are hurriedly making dinner.

With such a nice Bolognese on to simmer you are tempted to pour yourself a glass of wine, but you resist. You have a proposal/paper to read. An hour, later with the family settled into homework and television, you retire to the spare room that doubles as your study and open the laptop to read the proposal/paper. You are feeling tired and now a bit irritated that, five pages in, the paper/proposal is still drifting around. Why can't authors/applicants just say that they are doing? Why can't they be clear? If that was not bad enough, you keep having to re-read sentences that seem to be paragraphs long. Your mind begins to wander, and you start to feel anxious. It is all very well reading this proposal/paper, but what about that dissertation you are supposed to examine? Damn. That report was due yesterday, and it's already nine o'clock.

I could go on, but I suspect you have understood the point. Reviewers are busy professionals who are volunteering for this activity not because it pays well (they may receive a nominal amount, or book vouchers) but because they are members of an academic community, and this is what it involves. All academics depend on each other to freely review their book proposals, journal papers, funding proposals and promotions. It is a constant process of give and take. And, if you have not already, one day you may also be asked to review a paper or proposal. That is a great moment – welcome to the community and its hectic life of doing too many things at once, but generally on time and to the highest standard possible.

Understanding funders: stakeholders and reviewers

For funding applications, decisions often involve a panel of reviewers who meet for at least one full, and sometimes two or three subsequent, days. Well before that meeting, they will be asked to review a number of proposals, all of which have been through the preliminary sift by staff. Each member of the panel will be assigned a small number of proposals to read and assess in depth so that they are able to present their cases at the funding panel meeting, but all members are still expected to read and comment on proposals. This process is designed to produce comparison tables with points and comments awarded for each section of the proposal. An important point to note is that no panel member is an expert in every area being reviewed.

That is why it is hugely important to write your proposal in ways that can be understood by non-experts.

Who will be involved in decisions about a research proposal? There is no standard answer to that question, as it varies from funder to funder, but it can certainly be discovered. One way of so doing is often via a website. Another is by simply asking the question. The differences between reviewers can be significant but your question is always the same – what do they need, and how can I assure them that my research is worth their time and money?

Sometimes, at funding workshops I run, or at related meetings, someone will often nod and say, 'it's about playing the game'. I am not sure where they ever heard such nonsense, but I try to explain that they are wrong on several levels. First, there is no game and, second, anyone who thinks that understanding and responding to funders' criteria is some sort of prank they can play and emerge, victorious and unscathed, is deluded. Too many people, like you and me, are involved in the processes of assessing funding applications and we – academics – all do so in our spare time and for little, if any, tangible reward. We are reliant on each other and, increasingly, on front-line staff whose job it is to deal with the worst of the junk mail masquerading as a research proposal before it reaches our desks.

Many funders, like journals, place enormous emphasis on the role of their staff. When proposals come into the office, staff members look at them and become very active in the process of reviewing. They will weed out, sometimes with external advice, sometimes on their own, the weaker proposals. Some academics may raise an eyebrow here: how could an administrative staff member not trained in a specific subject area have the expertise to reject a proposal outright, before it has been seen by proper reviewers? Fortunately for the staff, the task is really not too difficult, as so many proposals are apparently haphazardly conceived, badly written, poorly expressed and bear no relationship to the criteria of the funder.

The proposals which make it past the staff screening process will then proceed to the process of peer review or, in the case of a charity, sometimes to their Board of Trustees. One such Trustee commented to me: 'As a Trustee it's really hard work', and she is grateful to the staff for making the initial shift. Proposals which are clear and match the charity's objectives are welcome, unlike those which, she said 'are just boring; some are very jargon-y, some are very worthy but it's not clear – what's the question?'.

For government funding, peer reviewers are experts in the field chosen to assess applications in the different subject areas. Many researchers talk about peer reviewers in hushed, revered tones, as if they are numinous creatures beyond human understanding. This assumption is quite inappropriate once you realize that peer reviewers are ordinary people, many of whom you probably know and meet at conferences every year. It is usually a simple process to find out who the peer reviewers are. Subject areas or specific schemes will often have panels and the membership of the panels is, in the case of a public body, publicly accessible.

It is more constructive to think of peer reviewers as people who have needs to be met, rather than as impartial gatekeepers to the academic body of knowledge. Find out the names of the peer reviewers and do an online search. Search engines like Google are all you need: enter their name and you will see immediately everything you need to know about them: links to their university home pages where you can read about their current areas of interest, expertise and research (and even view their picture! Now, how's that for looking human?), their career history where you can see what they did and maybe why, their publications list, and links to pages where you can read their papers and even do citation analysis. What might they be looking for? What do they sense in the body of knowledge is missing? Why would they want you to become a member of their academic community?

The researcher may look at the work purely from an individual or a team's point of view, whereas the funder must look at the researcher as a member in a community. This is something many people ignore, concentrating instead on how their project may enhance their own work or reputation but not how it may contribute to the programme as a whole. Commitment to the entire programme and its objectives and all those involved is a critical consideration. To be of value to the funder and its communities, the research must reflect the aims of the specific scheme within which an award is being sought, as well as the wider strategic aims of the funder. Knowing this and articulating it may make the final difference between equal, alpha-graded applications. This would apply equally to single research grants as to projects within large programmes.

Private sector organizations also have multiple stakeholders, including shareholders, staff, customers, the media, industry groups, legal and regulatory bodies, potential employees, pension fund investors, and competitors.

All of these relationships and interrelationships can be explored by reading the funder's strategic plan, which formulates and expresses corporate aims and objectives for activities that meet the aspirations, requirements and needs of those multiple stakeholders.

Understanding multiple needs

If, for example, you are contemplating submitting a proposal for a particular project programme within a public body, such as the ESRC or AHRC, your first question should be: how does this affect the needs of everyone involved? Research Councils have multiple stakeholders to satisfy. One set of stakeholders is the academic researchers and students they fund. Another set is the users of their research – in a sense, the customers and consumers of the research outputs – such as private or public bodies. Another group of stakeholders are policymakers – the funding bodies' own funding decision-makers, ultimately going to top levels in government. Yet another set is the media and wider public, who can have an influence, positively or negatively, on how politicians come to see research funding as a worthwhile investment as judged by their constituents.

The first stage of needs assessment is to become clear about the many different groups involved in what may appear to be a single funding organization. Every organization, of any kind, is involved in a hierarchy of relationships of which potential partners would be advised to become aware. That is why an important principle of needs analysis is the creation of a picture of the organization's relationships. Start at the lowest unit of analysis and work up and outwards.

Successful researchers become adept at finding out as much as possible about a potential funding partner before they decide to submit a proposal. It is tempting, when faced with the time pressures that any busy person has, to neglect doing detailed homework on a funding partner before completing an application. But as we have discussed, and will go on to discuss further, a research application is not an abstract entity, to be judged on 'its own merits'. It will be judged against how well it appears to deliver against a funder's objectives. Therefore, no assessment, or a superficial assessment of the funder's needs, is likely to lead to problems and disappointments further down the line.

One research manager at a UK university says that a good way to find out what people really want is to 'read between the lines'. The best way to learn what lies between the lines is to meet people. Information days, seminars, or conferences, offer good opportunities to talk with prospective funders and discover the nuances in the official regulations. Talking to a programme director, for example, may reveal more about what is being sought than the public guidelines can possibly cover.

A standard funding template for a research council gives the most important clues to its multiple stakeholders. Applicants are asked to fill out several sections, well beyond just their title and overview of the research. One section asks about how they will meet the needs of academic beneficiaries, and another of non-academic. In their funding guide (AHRC Research Funding Guide 2021) for example, the AHRC informs applicants that:

The Academic Beneficiaries section asks you to summarise how your research will benefit other researchers in your field and – where relevant – academic beneficiaries in other disciplines. Academic communication and dissemination plans should be elaborated further in your Case for Support. Academic Beneficiaries is a section to complete within the proposal form.

Following that advice, it turns to non-academic beneficiaries, asking applicants to:

Describe the proposed research in simple terms in a way that could be publicised to a general audience. Note that this summary may be published on the AHRC's website in the event that a grant is awarded. You should also summarise how the research will be beneficial to users who are within and beyond the academic research community, and how you intend on engaging with them.

As always, the best advice is often the most obvious: take time to research your prospective funder.

Summary

Authors and funding applicants need to recognize their position in a larger chain. By putting ourselves in the position of others in the chain we are more likely to see how the publishing or funding process benefits everyone. Of most immediate interest to the author or applicant are the funder's structure, editor, reviewer, and reader.

Writing may sometimes seem a lonely job, but next time you are sweating over a paper or proposal at midnight, consider the over-worked editor and reviewer who is doing much the same.

Action points

Here's an interesting exercise. Keep any direct mail that arrives at your home or office over the next week or so. When you have collected a small pile, sit down for an hour and pick out the two best communications and two worst. What makes the good ones good, and the bad ones bad? You will probably find that the good ones are good because they have, by accident or planning, somehow touched some need or desire or personal chord, and the bad ones are bad because they have studiously paid no attention whatsoever to who you are.

No, you are not being schooled as a direct mail campaign planner. But this exercise will help you pick up some tips on how to structure an unsolicited communication so that it has more chance of hitting the spot with the editor, and or their teams. And that's a useful skill.

Reference

AHRC Research Funding Guide (2021). 'Guidance on applying for AHRC research funding'. Available at: https://www.ukri.org/publications/ahrc-research-funding-guide/

10 CRITERIA FOR SUCCESS

How funders review

A successful funding application needs to address important questions: how do you make sure you have the right fit between yourself and the prospective funder, and how do you know if that message is getting through? It may be that you formulate a research proposal, or see an invitation to tender, and think 'Yes! That is such a good fit for me! I believe that right now, I really am the best-placed person in the world to do this specific piece of research'. You may be right, but several problems may nevertheless arise:

1. 300 other people also who believe they are the best in the world are applying for the same grant.
2. 200 of those really *are*, equally, the best suited in the world.
3. 150 of these have submitted accurate application forms and a proposal which matches the funder's specifications.
4. 100 of you have aligned your work to the aims and objectives of the funding agency, thereby emerging as a perfect candidate.
5. 50 of you have also created a faultless budget.
6. There is only enough money for 10 of you.

By paying attention to the key points reviewed in this chapter, particularly about matching the objectives between your proposed project and your prospective funder, you will increase your chances of being one of those applications at least being given serious consideration.

Criteria for successful proposals

The 'proposal' stage comes late in the process. By the time you get around to writing a proposal, you should be clear about who your funder is, what is required, and how you need to position your work.

DOI: 10.4324/9781003259718-12

Each proposal is unique. You may be creating this as a reply to an invitation to tender, or because you think your research matches a specific scheme. Alternatively, you may be submitting this after understanding a particular organization's issues, in which case this follows a lengthy exploration of someone's needs. There is, therefore, no single 'right' way to write a proposal – no pro forma or standard structure which can be simply photocopied, filled in, and submitted. The purpose of this chapter is to summarize some of the key points which winning proposals appear to have in common. Remember, always, that there are equally good proposals flooding into your prospective funder's office every day. Think of what the one funder says when it advises candidates in its guidance notes:

> To make your proposal stand out from the scores of other applications that will land on the assessors' desks, you will have to pay particular attention to the way that you write and present it.

When considering your proposal, look to see if it addresses the main issues:

- Research question
- Context
- Method
- Implications
- Value for money

The best proposals respond to those questions concisely and with timescales. Not addressing them is the most common cause, according to many funders, of application failure. The following points tend to appear on guidance notes indicating that a successful proposal will:

- pose research questions that will be addressed or problems that will be explored in the course of the research;
- show how those questions will be answered by achieving specific objectives;
- describe a research context for the research by specifying:
  - Why it is important that these particular questions should be answered, or problems explored.
  - What other research that has been or is being conducted in this area.
  - What particular contribution this particular project will make in that context to, for example, the body of knowledge, advancement of science, enhanced creativity, richer insights, or understanding;
- detail the selected research methods for addressing and answering the research questions, and the rationale for choosing those methods.

Let's look at those aspects in more detail

Research question

We have discussed in earlier chapters the nature of research questions and the need to focus. Former ESRC Research Director Chris Caswill told me that a problem with many proposals is that the topic is too broad. 'The topic itself must be researchable', he points out, adding that, unfortunately, 'Sometimes it is such a large canvas that it is impossible to do'.

Another research director remarked that 'You can have really good science on a really boring topic'. She described how there were several main aspects important to the charity she belonged to. The main one was focus: 'does it fit into the priorities that we've identified? Have they addressed the issue?'. Some researchers simply try their luck by slightly adapting what they really want to do to the apparent needs of the charity: 'they are trying it on because they're desperate for money, so they will slightly modify what they want to do to try to fit into our brief, and it may not work'.

A trustee of another charity offered a similar comment, speaking at the time during the global COVID-19 pandemic. Desperate to appear topical, 'some will shoe-horn COVID into their proposal when it's nothing to do with COVID', she remarked.

Context

The context referred to here is both the background of the research question and also the context of the funding partner and their community. We have already explored the need to understand who the partner is, who their stakeholders are, and how you fit into that community and can enrich it. Now, in your proposal, is the time to articulate that and make it clear to the funder that not only have you taken the time and effort to find out but know how to work within that context.

This book has referred to funders' guidance notes and websites. One of the interesting features of websites is that the owner can review and assess the navigation behaviour of those who visit them. Website owners review that kind of information frequently in an effort to improve their sites, but it is also used to get a better picture about the behaviour and characteristics of those who visit them.

Sharon Witherspoon, then deputy director of the Nuffield Foundation, told administrators at a research funding symposium that it is evident many researchers do not bother to find out enough about the organization: 'we know because we can see how far they have gone into our website. Many people do not go far enough'. They do not, in other words, develop 'in-house scrutiny'.

How can you demonstrate in your proposal that you have taken the trouble to do that 'in-house scrutiny'? Some of your scrutinies will become obvious in the way that you frame your questions and situate them within the context. You can go further by using the actual language of the funder and referring to, for example, their strategic aims or points of ethos by quoting them directly. Don't just do the homework; be seen to be doing it.

Method

Having thought about the context, it is necessary for the proposal not to allow that to drive out the aspect which should form the heart of the proposal: method. And yet, many applicants neglect it. This often includes experienced researchers who assume that their experience alone will reassure the funder that they know how to collect and analyze data: do not take such things for granted; articulate your approach in detail.

A research director told me that:

> at one stage I started drawing up a kind of check list of important points, and one of them is: if the background and elaboration of the problem is longer than the methods and the aims, then it goes in the bin. This is a slight exaggeration, but I think there are, more seriously, two things. There's the kind of focus of the issue – And then I think the other thing is how people are proposing to do the work and even though I think proposals have got better over the last few years, we still get an awful lot that are under-specified in terms of the method.

Although this point has been dealt with in earlier chapters, it is worth repeating here as it is so often given as the primary reason for application failure. Describe your method in as much detail as possible. This is obvious, and yet often overlooked by poorly considered proposals. Asked for his 'top tips' for application success, former ESRC Research Director Chris Caswill stressed that insufficiently describing the method is often the single most frequent cause of failure: 'These are applications to do research, so it is extremely important to discuss the research in the application', he wryly remarked.

Some applicants only offer a brief discussion of the subject area and a literature review. The methods must be appropriate and well-designed for the question, but simply mentioning that is not enough. Sufficient detail is necessary to convince the funder the methods have been designed and defined and the applicant knows how to carry them out. 'The majority of proposals which get close yet fail, do so because research methods are either inappropriate or ill-defined', Caswill said.

How can you be sure your proposal adequately covers method? A checklist of common methodology faults may include:

- Vague research design and lack of clarity
- Poor information about methods of data collection
- Weak discussion of data analysis
- Unrealistic timescales, often related to under-budgeting

The last point often surprises applicants who may erroneously think that an inexpensive proposal is a winning proposal, when in practice poor budgeting often results from poor consideration of method. Do you really think, for example, you can expect one research assistant to carry out six interviews a day for six months? Better to budget for two researchers than appear that you have not understood the implications of your research methods. Funders are not looking for cheap work, but work that is realistic and represents value for money.

If, for example, you are proposing a quantitative survey, say what it will look like. If you are going to conduct focus groups, say why and how you will analyze them. 'I think everyone wants to do focus groups these days', a Research Director said 'They may be very trendy, but they are difficult to do properly and analyze. Some people do not give enough background about this'.

Make sure that methods are tied explicitly to aims: some research proposals do not link the research question or aims to appropriate methods. The question, for example, may involve quantitative evidence, but the approach, in contrast, centres on qualitative methods. That may not be a suitable match but, at the very least, will require significant justification.

Writing style

Many proposals which are well structured and considered fail to convey the key points. This often happens when people try to write in a more complicated and supposedly sophisticated style than is necessary. The best way around that problem is to focus on the readers and remember that many of them may not be experts in your field.

Engage with the reader

In the discussion in Chapter 4 on what is meant by 'good' research, one of the points which many researchers emphasized strongly was the notion of accessibility and engagement; that good research is accessible to all sorts of people and engages people. The involvement of the person, perhaps even a non-scholar, reading the research is part of what makes it good.

So, how can you make sure your work engages people? Firstly, you have to understand the people with whom you are communicating, but if you reviewed carefully the points in the previous chapters, you will have done that. Next, you have to make sure you are using language and tone that ease understanding. There are three main pitfalls to avoid.

Verbosity

Why take 200 words to say something when 50 will do? If you originally thought the section was only going to need 200 words, why are you still writing after 750? It is probably because you have become carried away by your own thoughts and lost touch with what the reader needs. You may have become unsure of what you are trying to say, so you keep circling around, avoiding coming to a conclusion.

To keep the focus, review the criteria. Remember what you had already worked out. Discipline yourself to write less than you want and remember that reviewers are unimpressed by long, turgid sentences.

Jargon

As one funder noted, 'when you read an application written in jargon you know it covers up messy thinking'. Jargon is a private shorthand that sometimes helps us communicate quickly to those who know the same jargon. We may be familiar with it, our colleagues may be familiar with it, but the reader may be lost. Worse, readers may suspect that you are deliberately obscuring something, or trying to be intimidating. It never ends well when people try to make reviewers feel, or appear, stupid.

Read your material carefully and ask yourself whether your readers will understand. If you have any doubt, change the word or phrase into user-friendly language. Examine the concepts that you have borrowed. Best of all, have someone outside your field read it.

Is it likely that people unfamiliar with your work will understand? Most journals and funders, however specialized, are unwilling to accept papers or proposals only decipherable by a small group of specialists. Be especially careful of acronyms: always spell them out the first time.

Impressive words

Use words to express, not to impress. The best writing is always the simplest and the clearest. Is there really a good reason to use that longer or more complex word? The best way to avoid using the wrong word is to keep your words as simple as possible. Use your dictionary but throw away your thesaurus. Too often, people consult a thesaurus to find a bigger, more important-sounding word for the more common, more familiar word. If you are going to use a thesaurus, use it the other way round, to move from the complex to the simple.

Testing your paper

Finally, put your work to the test. Ask a colleague or friend to help you. It does not matter if they are familiar with your subject area; indeed, it may be preferable that they are not. Ask them to assess your paper or proposal by browsing it quickly, using five criteria:

1. **Purpose:** clearly stated on the first page?
2. **Key points:** logically flowing from point to point with signposting, such as subheadings, introductions and conclusions to sections?
3. **Implications:** clearly specified, with special attention to who the implications are for and what readers can do next?
4. **Readability:** jargon-free, familiar words, reasonably short sentences, easy-to-follow theme?
5. **Appeal:** Would they go back and read the paper or proposal more thoroughly?

This exercise models what we readers – you, they and I – do all the time. We scan, we browse, we sift. Readers want access to the right information they can understand and use. Given a choice between a turgid, vague, obscure paper or proposal, and a paper or proposal which reveals what you are looking for, which one would you choose?

It is hard to improve upon what George Orwell (2013) did to illustrate the importance of how clear language links to clear thinking. His advice is that if you do not know what to say, use as many syllables and vague words as possible. He offered an example from the Biblical book of *Ecclesiastes* to make the point:

> I returned and saw under the sun, that the race is not to the swift, nor the battle to the strong, neither yet bread to the wise, nor yet riches to men of understanding, nor yet favour to men of skill; but time and chance happeneth to them all.

Few could say they do not get the author's point, but how clear would be the meaning if we read instead Orwell's own parody of how the passage would be written in 'modern English' (or, as we might say, 'academic English'):

> Objective considerations of contemporary phenomena compels the conclusion that success or failure in competitive activities exhibits no

tendency to be commensurate with innate capacity, but that a considerable element of the unpredictable must be invariably taken into account.

In describing what your proposal or paper is about it is useful to bear in mind the standard checklist given for story-writing in primary school:

- Who
- What
- Where
- When
- Why
- How

Try to keep your paragraphs short and use devices such as bullet points to break up the text.

It is also worth remembering that a picture may indeed paint a thousand words. Many funders and successful researchers recommend using diagrams. This can quickly capture and convey important information. When I interviewed Prof. Rosalind Edwards at South Bank University, about her five-year ESRC-funded programme on Families and Social Capital, she said that her use of diagrams was one of the strengths of her proposal. She wanted to demonstrate that the programme would be well managed through a team structure which reflected the aims and objectives of the programme. This point was made by the ESRC in its guidance notes, advising applicants to use diagrams and other graphic devices whenever possible as they help get points across and overcome language barriers.

Check your proposal for grammar and spelling, letting other people read it so that the errors you cannot see are spotted. As Peter Brown, then Secretary of the British Academy remarked at a research funding symposium: 'Assessors take a dim view of illiterate applications'.

Always keep to the word length. If the funder asks for two hundred words, do two hundred but no more. Exceeding the recommended length is annoying for the funder because it makes it more difficult to compare proposals. It also reflects badly on the researcher who apparently is not thinking clearly enough. After all, it is harder to write 200 well-constructed and concise words than 800.

Talk to them!

If you are uncertain about any aspect of the proposal, just ask. Readers will by now be familiar with this mantra running throughout this book: 'talk to them!'.

One successful researcher pointed out that academics may not ask for help because it is not part of the academic culture. Senior academics are, of course, expected to know everything. In their experience the best approach is to develop a rapport with people within the funding organization:

> There is that grey area and you've got to know who you're dealing with. Don't send things anonymously. Find out who's involved in the process. Develop a contact, rapport – ask him, seek advice. Don't be too confident in your ideas. Everybody's got good ideas and try to learn from other people's experience. A lot of people prefer to have all of nothing rather than half of something and that's a big problem because they're academics. You know, we traditionally don't like asking for help. I think that's a key point.

Internal review

In the almost three decades since the first edition of this research was published, the roles of university Research Managers and Administrators at universities have become better recognized and represented, particularly by their professional association, ARMA UK (n.d.).

Rather than being looked down upon as inconvenient barriers for academics to somehow avoid, they have become a more integral part of the research planning, proposing, and managing process. As they should. One research manager I interviewed was clear about the benefits of taking a fresh look at the proposal, and emphasized the importance of internal review systems:

> Once you have written your Case for Support, you need to stand back from it. Academics are close to their work and sometimes forget that this is not an academic paper, but a sales pitch. Often, this doesn't come across. Be responsive to their requirements; know the sponsors' regulations inside-out.

This requires a fine balance at times between complying with the regulations of the external sponsor or funder, and the academic's needs. Research managers and administrators can help review proposals to see if they achieve that balance. Many academics under-estimate the role and potential of university research administrators. Some refuse to admit that an administrator outside a subject area could possibly have anything useful to say about a proposal, ignoring the fact that such people see more proposals and more responses from funding agencies in an average day than most academics see in a year.

How can academics work with research administrators in their efforts to submit winning applications? A common response to that question was 'Involve us earlier!' It is far from unusual, I was told, for an academic to come to the support office in the morning with a funding application which has to be sent later that same day. It would be a help if things were not always last-minute, although administrators are often quick to point out that organization and micro-planning techniques are not attributes normally associated with academics: 'they just don't seem to think that way!'

If the application is successful, the research administrators will work set up systems to administer the grant, working closely with personnel and payroll departments as well as the researchers. People need to be paid on time, invoices sent at appropriate intervals to the funding agency and the final reports submitted.

What can the researchers do to help the administrators keep the project running smoothly? It may help to realize that a support office will have hundreds of grants running at any one time, with often only a few members of staff to administer them. The last thing they want are surprises. The administrators I spoke to were all keen to be kept involved. Changes might occur during the course of a project, and it helps to keep the administrators informed. Sometimes, for example, researchers might apply for an extension and forget to tell the administrator or decide to spend more or less time on particular phases of the project which may have implications for allocations.

One administrator recently entertained a group which was meeting to discuss research funding with an amusing, if somewhat bizarre, story about an academic at her institution who came to the administration office to seek information about creating a budget for a proposal. The administrator read through the proposal and noticed that it said little about the research methodology. When she helpfully pointed out that funding agencies normally like to see discussion and detail about method, the academic rejoined, 'well, this is just the way we do research here and if the ESRC doesn't like it, tough'.

They didn't, of course.

Apart from the Research Office, many institutions also insist that proposals go through wider academic review within the university, sometimes via proprietary platforms such as *Worktribe*. Other institutions will use department academic staff to review each other's proposals less formally. Whichever method is used, the salient point is the same: any potential research proposal can be usefully reviewed internally before it is submitted. As the number of proposals being submitted increases, many funders are insisting that this is so. They call it 'demand management'. I prefer to call it sensible scrutiny.

As a final review, it is wise to check the proposal against the main criteria affecting most proposals.

1. Articulates problem accurately.
2. Provides appropriate background.
3. Manageable within the time.
4. Cost-effective.
5. Linked to defined outcomes.
6. Seen to make a contribution to the field.
7. Clear methodology.
8. Concise writing.
9. Demonstrates right team approach.
10. Has credible academic supervision.

When your proposal is submitted, it will be sent to reviewers using a template similar to this one, encapsulating all the above points.

1. Scientific quality.

Comment on the aims/objectives of the proposed research, including its scientific importance, the innovative aspects and the clarity of the problem. Opinion on the aims/objectives of the proposed research, including its scientific importance, the innovative aspects and the clarity of the problem?

2. Method/Research design.

Comment on the adequacy of the approach/method in view of the aims of the proposal, in particular as for its originality or innovative aspects. If applicable, comment on the multidisciplinary and interdisciplinary character of the proposal. What is your opinion on the adequacy of the approach/methodology in view of the aims of the proposal, in particular as for its originality or innovative aspects?

3. Research/work plan.

Comment on the feasibility and soundness of the research plan. Is the timetable realistic? Do the applicants provide adequate review points? Are their alternative or back-up plans if something changes?

   4. Research team.

Comment on the expertise, experience and qualifications of the research team. This will relate here to the previous results of the applicant, the research team and the proposed research assistant. What is the adequacy of the research team? Do they have a record of co-operation with other researchers in this field? How feasible is it, in terms of experience, supervision and logistic facilities, that they will complete the project successfully?

   5. Relevance.

What is your opinion on the (scholarly/scientific) relevance of the proposed research, including the transfer of knowledge, and its topical interest? What is your opinion on the societal/cultural/technical relevance of the proposed research?

   6. If the proposal is for a research Programme, containing a variety of projects within it, there are different considerations. A Programme usually consists of several projects, often including doctoral or post-doctoral staff. The purpose of a Programme is to create a synthesis amongst the individual projects to create a surplus or added value.

What is your opinion of the value of the programmatic approach, the relationship between the programme and the projects defined within the research programme, and the inter-relationship between the individual projects? Please comment on how the Programme is related to, and, if appropriate, embedded with relevant universities or research institutions.

Final assessment

Please summarize or briefly comment (point by point) on the Strengths/Opportunities and Weaknesses/Potential threats of the proposed research given above?

Reviewers will then be asked to award overall scores, which typically look something like this:

I will conclude this section with a selection of funders' quotes from their guidance notes and websites I have collected over the years. I want to share them here not because they repeat the same points as above, but because the writing conveys a tone: these are funders who know exactly who should apply

A+   Highest quality, significance and recommendation for funding: The applicant and research proposal are of the highest quality. The proposed research is at the forefront internationally and will have substantial and innovative impact.
Funding is highly recommended

A   High quality, significance, and recommendation for funding
The applicant and/or research proposal are of a high quality. The proposed research is internationally competitive and will make a significant contribution.
Funding is recommended

B   Good quality and significant
The applicant and/or research proposal are of a good quality. The proposed research will make a valuable contribution but has some minor weaknesses.
Funding is recommended only if ample resources are available

UF   Unsuccessful in this form
The applicant and/or research proposal are of sufficient quality. The proposed research will provide some new insights but has significant weaknesses.
Funding of the proposal in its present form is not recommended

U   Unsuccessful
The applicant and/or research proposal lack sufficient quality. The proposed research is weak in its scientific and/or methodological approach, and/or repeats other work.
Funding is not recommended

and how. Readers may find it astonishing that any applicant would fail to grasp the funder's requirements. The title for this section is self-explanatory.

Stating the obvious

A certain wistful tone creeps into the guidance notes given a funder (the examples below have been anonymised) below, which suggests that too many applicants have not bothered with such basic advice as reading the guidance notes. Instead, they may take a rather perfunctory attitude to 'filling in' an application form, rather than see it as a masterpiece of relationship management:

> **Read the rules and the guidance notes** attached to the application form which are designed to help you through the 'filling in' process. This cannot be over-stressed; familiarising yourself with the content of the Research Funding Guidelines may seem tedious but will help you to avoid basic mistakes which at best will require clarification with office staff and at worst may prejudice chances of success. [Emphasis theirs]

Further advice is given on how to write proposals, ending with a sentence which suggests that weary assessors have had a few too many late nights struggling with poorly constructed proposals:

> do take the trouble to check spelling, grammar and punctuation. These are all part of the quality of presentation and **presentation matters!** [Emphasis theirs]

And then, just in case you did not get it first time, make no mistake…

> Get your proposal in on time. If you miss the deadline – even by a minute it will be rejected. To be on the safe side, try to submit your proposal at least a week ahead of the deadline…

Puzzled as to why your brilliant application was rejected? The a funder explains why this might have been. It is obvious, of course:

> Staff will read your proposal to check that it meets the basic funding criteria. Has it been submitted on time? Does it meet the programme's objectives? Does it contain sufficient partners? The summary of your proposal will play an important part in helping them answer these questions. […] around 15 per cent of proposals were rejected at this stage. If you fall at this hurdle, your co-ordinator will be notified immediately.

No surprises here. Nothing hidden, nothing to trip you up or trick you. Remember, they want to give their money to good applicants. But to qualify as a good applicant, you have to jump some basic hurdles. Here's another one; the a funder's advice on basic rules of organization:

> When the call is announced, you must obtain a copy of the relevant information pack which will provide all the necessary details and funding criteria, as well as the application forms. Every partner should read the documents thoroughly and suggest appropriate alterations to the proposal in the light of any changes to the programme's objectives. These should be taken into account in the co-ordinator's final draft, which must be signed off by all the partners.

Another example of having to state the obvious is given by the AHRC whose first point about eligibility – and the entire premise of this book – could not be clearer: the application, it stated, will be eligible only if it complies with the Council's definition of research and if the subject matter falls within its remit.

The need to match the funder's needs is also top of the list from the Joseph Rowntree Foundation:

> Full details of the Foundation's interests and those of each Committee are given in the Current Priorities section. When looking at each proposal, the relevant Committee will consider:
>
> - the relevance of the topic to the Foundation's priorities;
> - whether the work will offer new insights or developments;
> - the soundness and appropriateness of how the work will be done (for research projects this covers both the research design, the methods and the analysis);
> - whether partnerships with relevant organisations and service users are in place where these are important;
> - the ability of the staff to carry out the work and complete on time;
> - the likely policy and practice implications;
> - a thorough approach to dissemination.

The British Academy also takes a rather pointed approach, both to eligibility and punctuality. Academics may like to work to last-minute deadlines, but the clear message here is that the Academy does not like to be rushed. It even highlights in bold, for those of you who did not pay attention, who is eligible. Helpfully, it also suggests that people at different levels of academic status are eligible:

> Most awards are made to staff employed in universities and other institutions of higher education, but applicants are not restricted by either academic or employment status. Rather, they must show that they are seeking support for advanced research at postdoctoral or equivalent level. **PhD Candidates are not eligible to apply**, whether or not the project is related to the topic of their thesis. Awards are not available for the support of courses of study leading to professional qualifications. Awards cannot be made retrospectively; applications must be made in time for them to be considered well before the research or other work to which they relate is due to begin. [Emphasis theirs]

Journal criteria

The same people who review funding applications will likely also review journal papers. Some may be members of the journal's editorial board, while others may be selected because they are known to be experts in their fields. Like the questions posed to potential funding reviewers, the journal's reviewers – or, as they are more commonly called, referees – are hard-working academic volunteers. Their details form part of a database that organizes them according to discipline, method, region, or other relevant data.

Referees are notified by email that a paper has arrived for their review and, if they accept the invitation, are directed to the journal's site from where they can download the paper and see the criteria. When they reach their judgement, they will fill out a form with questions inviting their opinion.

Referees will consider any paper first in terms of how it matches the journal's objectives. As discussed particularly in Chapter 8, accurately targeting journals is the most important step authors can take. The next is to ensure the paper is clear and its purpose, and implications, well-articulated. Most journals have similar checklists for referees: consider these points and visualize the referee sitting at their computer reading your paper with the checklist open to guide their thinking. Next time you think you have completed your paper, read it like the referee would:

1. Is the title appropriate, giving a clear idea about the content using words likely to enable visibility and access?
2. Does the paper have clear aims?
3. Are the paper's aims achieved?
4. Is the contribution made in this paper new and substantial, either in argument, findings or method?
5. If it does not propose new work, what is its purpose? For example, does it competently replicate existing work in order to further support or modify?
6. Does the paper have a clear structure?
7. Is the theoretical framework, method, and findings aligned?
8. Are the methods appropriate?
9. Is it clearly written, avoiding jargon and cliches?

One point above deserves a little more explanation: the title. Before you submit a paper with a cute and catchy title, consider the importance of what publishers and librarians call 'discoverability'. As a researcher, you might recall what it was like to do a literature search by keyword. Hold that thought as you write 'Rocking for the future' as the title of a paper on how contemporary musicians are increasingly focusing their attention on climate change.

Some journals helpfully provide specific guidance on titles. The *South African Journal of Economic and Management Sciences* (*SAJEMS*) (n.d.), for example, advises authors to follow a specific format: 'Specific, descriptive, concise, and comprehensible to readers outside the field. Max 95 characters (including spaces)'.

Referees are then asked to draw a general conclusion, noting whether they feel the paper is making an outstanding, moderate, little, or no contribution to the readership.

Their final recommendation will fall into one of the following categories:

- Accept as is.
- Accept subject to minor revisions.
- Revise and resubmit for further consideration (acceptance not guaranteed).
- Reject.

Here is an extract from a referee report I wrote for a journal, with several words deleted in order to protect confidentiality:

1. Good statement of the purpose of the paper at the outset, well-structured, and well-written.
2. This paper begins with an interesting case of how a debate about [...] analyzed primarily according to [...] models. While some expert readers may find this useful, as it stands, I am not convinced it would engage the more general reader of [...]
3. The author needs to situate the paper better – either as a single, worked example of how [...] works in practice, or as a more theoretically robust paper.
4. Its main weakness is the Authors' failure to move from describing a single case to making wider, generalized claims.
5. Another main problem is the Authors' largely unsubstantiated claim of an impoverished existing theoretical base in the field.
6. There is a lack of disciplinary roots. Which analytical framework is being used? There is a smattering of unconnected source material.

Recommendation: Rejection

But referees do far more than just make yes or no decisions on papers. Referees and editors often work hard to help an author become publishable. Most papers that come into a journal's review stream are 'publishable' somewhere, at least after sufficient revision, even if that 'somewhere' is often not the first journal to which the paper is submitted (and, I suggest, recall the advice given here in Chapter 8 about targeting journals). Consider the revision process as a journey, where the distance from current draft to publishable article can be covered via several different paths, with referees sometimes not agreeing on what the needed revisions should be. The editor's task is then to ascertain what areas in a paper need revision, what direction those revisions should take, and assess whether the current paper (and its author) is up for the journey. Thus, an editor has a substantial impact on the scholarship that appears in print by shaping papers through promoting some revisions, offering feedback on what works and what does not. As one editor told me:

> An editor cannot make a bad paper into a classic, but she or he can make an okay paper into a good article, and a good paper into a great one. When each new issue of the journal comes out, on time, with articles that I have often helped to shape significantly, the overwhelming emotion is pride.

The editor continued to explain that while it may be easy to think that editors do their jobs by publishing papers that they like and rejecting those they do not, this is not true – nor even possible. According to the 'norms of scholarly fairness', the reviewing process solicits anywhere from one to four external assessments of each paper. This means that the editor cannot really be an effective editor 'if one isn't somewhat eclectic and broad-minded in one's approach'.

In the next chapter I will explore in more detail how to respond to referees' recommendations for revision.

Summary

In writing papers or proposals, bear in mind the obvious points that apply to both:

- Is this the right funder/journal – has the funder's or journal's needs been properly researched; has 'in-house scrutiny' been undertaken?
- The research question – is it clear? Have you addressed the issue?
- The context – have you stated the background and how your research fits?
- The method – is it described in detail, matching the question and aims? Is it realistic?
- So what? – why does your research matter?

Make sure your writing style is clear and as simple as possible. Use diagrams where appropriate. Make sure you check your grammar and spelling very carefully. You are presenting a communication document.

Try to engage with the funding body or journal in your work, to demonstrate that you have read and acted on their notes for guidance. Someone has spent a long time writing them. It is likely to be well received if you can show that you have responded to them.

Finally, be conscious of using your institution's internal review systems properly. Research administrators can be highly valued colleagues in the successful submissions of proposals to funding bodies.

Action points

1. Use one of the templates above to assess, section by section, your draft paper or proposal.
2. Read one or two papers from your target journal and assess how the authors have produced a paper that matches the key criteria as shown above.

References

ARMA UK (n.d.). The Association. Available at https://arma.ac.uk/about-arma/about-us/

Orwell, George (2013). *Politics and the English language.* London: Penguin.

South African Journal of Economic and Management Sciences (SAJEMS) (n.d.). Submission Guidelines. Available at: https://sajems.org/index.php/sajems/pages/view/submission-guidelines

PART III
PAPERS, PROPOSALS, AND BEYOND

11 WRITING BETTER, WRITING FASTER

Your plan

Let's start with a review of where we have got so far. By now you may have worked through the ideas contained in the earlier chapters and are ready to work on the article or proposal itself. Take a few moments now to summarize progress.

This is also the time to force yourself to appraise your work through the readers' eyes. Step back and evaluate what the reader needs to know. If you do not, you will find your reader is unable to share with you the excitement and value of your work. Once confusion sets in, there is no communication, just a one-way monologue, as one reviewer noted:

> Although the English is good, I found it difficult to follow. The authors are too close to the topic to be able to describe in terms easily understandable to those not familiar with the techniques.

Think of a paper or a proposal as a dialogue with the reader where you seek to answer your reader's questions before or as they arise. Any paper or funding Case for Support should have a beginning, middle, and an end, evident to the reader, but also *en route* through the paper, the reader needs to know not only what is being said at the time, but also where it is leading. Some may argue that a more individualistic and idiosyncratic style is preferable, but the truth is, any communication's objective is to achieve understanding with the reader, and unless one is a very skilled writer indeed, this is best achieved by following some clear signposted steps. The more idiosyncratic we become the more barriers we may raise. People who become too self-conscious of their personal style begin to lose respect for the reader's needs.

A sensible structure will have a strong beginning to explain to the reader:

- The purpose of your paper/proposal: what is it about?

DOI: 10.4324/9781003259718-14

- Why it is important (so what?).
- To whom it is important (who cares?).

Once the reader is oriented to those questions, another obvious one arises. Who are you? What they need now is background. Explain who you are and why you tackled the problem. Remind them of the reasons everyone in the field has been searching for such answers.

This should be an easy section to write. You are aware of the problem and what other people have said about it. The purpose of this section is to provide context and lend credibility to what you say and reassure the reader. Now the readers are genuinely interested, but they have moved into a more critical phase. They are asking questions such as: how did you decide to go about it? This is resonant, again, of funders who have described their frustration with authors who do not describe their method.

In a classic research student's textbook, *The Management of a Student Research Project* (Sharp, Peters and Howard 2017), the authors gave the following advice to authors of research papers, based on the reader's thought process:

> *Question–answer*: Every time you generate a question – 'But, what is the critical variable?' – the reader will expect an answer to follow quickly.
>
> *Problem-solution*: When you describe a problem the reader wants to know what the solution is or, if there is not one, why not.
>
> *Cause-effect/effect-cause*: Cause and effect – if this, then that – must be linked, in whatever order you present it.
>
> *General-specific*: When making a general or sweeping statement the reader will want to see how you qualify it with specific examples and evidence. The converse is also true. When you make specific statements, the reader will want to know if that comment can be generalised. Adding to the body of knowledge usually requires generalisation, but not to the point of obscurity.

Some journals guide authors to follow a specific structure with key attributes. The *Journal of East African Natural History* (Nature Kenya/East African Natural History Society 2022), for example, provides a suggested structure:

> Headings: the following format is preferred: 'Abstract, Introduction, Material and Methods, Results, Discussion, Acknowledgments, References'. A 'Description of the study area' may be inserted after the

Introduction if this is deemed necessary. Other headings, although discouraged, are acceptable if justified by the material to be presented. All headings should be typed on a separate line from the subsequent text. Main headings should be to the left of the page, in bold, capital letters.

Writing a synopsis of the paper or proposal is a good place to start, whether or not it becomes appropriate to send it to an editor or funder. A synopsis will help clarify your own thoughts by forcing you to articulate the key points. Before you start you need to know where the article or proposal will be sent. This seems to be an obvious point, but too many would-be authors simply write their paper or proposal and think about where to send it later. As discussed several times in this book, and practicality in Chapter 8, targeting the correct journal or funder is your most important task.

Writing a synopsis will ensure that you structure, angle, and write your paper or proposal suitably for your audience. By the time you finish this section, you will be completely familiar with the journal or funder and will have no lingering doubts about who these people are and what they want. You will also be clear about how your article or proposal will meet the journal's or funder's objectives because you will create a statement under each heading declaring exactly how you will be complying with the objectives.

To prepare for this, before writing a synopsis make notes against the headings we have already discussed. Try to keep the notes to only a sentence or two – 20 words or less is ideal. Make sure that your thoughts are clear about headings 1 and 2 before proceeding to the next stage.

1. Purpose
2. Implications
3. Target audience

- Editorial objectives or funder's aims (take these from the journal's Notes for Authors or funder's website); add new points you have found from reading the editorials or case studies about funded projects.
  - o Editorial or funder pen-sketch: a short description of the main editor or funder: position, length of term, area of interest.
  - o A short description of relevant section editors.
  - o Main reviewers likely to read your manuscript and any clues you have about them.
- Style (length and tone):
  - o Take from Notes for Authors or funder's guidelines.

o Add new points from editorials, reviewers' checklist, from reading the journal, reviewing successful proposals.
- Target readership:
  o Take from the Notes for Authors.
  o Add new points from editorials and reviewer's checklist or pro forma.
  o Note what benefits the editor and readers are seeking.

Ask yourself essential questions about your proposed paper or proposal:

- What wider principles emerged (or will emerge) from your research?
- How can people in your field use (or could use) it?
- Can people in other fields use it?
- How can other researchers take your work forward?
- How can your research be applied in practice?
- Who is able to apply your findings?
- What might they do?
- When and where might it be done?
- How might they approach it?

The answers to some of these questions may be 'do not know' or 'not applicable'. Which ones do apply, and what are your answers?

Quality criteria: how will your paper be judged?

- Evidence of relative importance of quality variables:
  o Take from Notes for Authors.
  o Add new points from the critical reading of papers.

List in order of importance, for example originality, research rigour, practical applications, contribution to body of knowledge, clarity, internationality, and others you think count. The reviewers and ultimately the readers of different journals may have slightly different views about what is important. Know this first, or risk coming across the reviewer who wrote:

> The results seem to be presented in a rather curious way, with apparently quite important findings virtually ignored while less satisfactory findings are highlighted.

How will you meet the objectives and satisfy the needs you have defined above? Try to summarize what you now know into simple statements that show how you will attend to your findings. For example, if rigour of research method ranks as the most important variable for a target readership seeking new research approaches, you might write something like this:

Criterion: Research methodology: My plan for approaching the research was…; I identified my sample group by…; I tested the sample by…; I chose to conduct semi-structured interviews because…; and so on.

Alternatively, if the quality of the contribution to the body of knowledge is most important, you will have to emphasize the literature review and therefore might note something like this:

Criterion: Evaluative review of relevant literature Note the term 'evaluative'. As I described earlier, the essence of the literature review is its analysis, not simply its summary. Use phrases to indicate…; that I focused on key theories by…; I chose the following sources of information…

Now follow the four points in Chapter 7 about reviewing and evaluating the literature:

1. Summarize
2. Synthesize
3. Analyze
4. Authorize

Following that review, write your fifth point:

5. **Interpret and justify.** All your work eventually leads to interpreting and justifying your findings. Make notes about how you will do this. Do not attempt to fake it here. If your findings were not all you expected, say so. If they do not quite prove the point you hoped to make, do not march grimly along your predetermined path. Wave the white flag and tell them how you might get it better next time. Otherwise, you will fall into the trap of so many who are desperate for publication at any cost – trying to fool the reviewer. Do not bother. You don't want to incite the reviewer who said:

The interpretation of some of the results is heroic bordering on the implausible.

The five points above cover the main issues any author must consider before planning the paper in any more detail. It sets the frame for what is to come and allows you to write a brief synopsis of the chapter. The synopsis is to help you structure your paper and therefore should be kept simple and short. Use the criteria we have already discussed to draw attention to the paper's value to the reader.

Writing a synopsis

Now that you have thought through the above points, discipline yourself to restrict your synopsis to a maximum of two pages. Once you have thought through and made notes on the issues above, it will take a very short time to write 1,000 words or so. The following headings will guide you:

- **Target readership.** 'The paper [or proposal[is designed for researchers in the field of applied mathematics who are seeking innovative approaches.'
- **Statement of aims.** 'The paper [or proposal] focuses on the problem currently faced by researchers and shows how, using a new approach, some of the obstacles are removed.'
- **Implications.** 'The paper [or proposal] reveals how researchers can use the new technique in the following circumstances to obtain the desired results…'
- **Treatment.** 'The paper [or proposal's Case for Support] will be 6,000 words long and cover the following sections in this order [or insert headings recommended by funder]: introduction, background, evaluative review of relevant literature, method, review of method, findings, analysis, implications, conclusions, references.'
- **Availability.** 'The paper [for funded research] will be ready [or insert timetable or follow funder's guidance notes] for delivery to the journal in three weeks.'
- **Author(s).** 'The authors [applicants] are professor and senior lecturer respectively at the University of West Chicago, whose research has been funded by the Institute of Applied Mathematics. Please see brief biographical details attached.'

The synopsis can now act as your guide for creating the detailed outline to follow and to circulate to joint authors and other colleagues. It sets clearly the intent and value of the paper and demonstrates that the hard homework of preparation is finished. In the order above, it also demonstrates that you have thought through the paper from the reader's perspective and have successfully matched the reader's, or funder's, needs with your own needs and resources.

You can find out whether or not an editor or funder wants a synopsis by checking the Notes for Authors or Applicants. More often than not, the editor or funder will want to see the completed paper, or proposal, in preference to a synopsis. After all, if you have done your research on the journal or the funder, it should be obvious that the paper or proposal is, in principle, suitable. This can reassure you that the paper or proposal will meet the first objective of sending it to a journal or funder: getting it into the review stream.

The synopsis and the key points above are critical for your own clarity. There is, after all, no fear of confused writing if the thinking is clear. Another good way to clarify your message at this state is to write the paper's abstract.

Depending on the submission method, some journals ask for a cover letter. The *South African Journal of Economic and Management Sciences* (*SA-JEMS*), for example, specifies in its note for authors that 'The compulsory cover letter forms part of a submission and must be submitted together with all the required'. In this case, a short letter based on an abstract or synopsis is designed to allow editorial staff to judge quickly whether the paper is suitable for the journal and, if it is, to consider which reviewers might be most appropriate.

Overview

The author guidelines include information about the types of articles received for publication and preparing a manuscript for submission. Other relevant information about the journal's policies and the reviewing process can be found under the about section. All forms need to be completed in English.

Writing an abstract

An abstract is a short summary of your article or proposal which contains all the key points it makes. Abstracts are normally printed at the head of the article, or in the relevant proposal section, or all together on an abstract page.

Reflecting on her lengthy tenure as a journal editor, Marie Cornwall (2010) offers aspiring authors advice on getting published. She suggests authors think carefully about their paper title, and abstract, because even before a reader gets a chance to see it, the paper must enter the review stream. It is the title and abstract that potential reviewers see before they decide whether to accept an invitation to review. That is why they need to be informative, not clever and catchy, she advises: 'The better the match between a good reviewer and your manuscript, the better the review'. The first clue about whether the paper will be worth a reviewer's time is the title and abstract because, she says: 'a poorly written abstract signals a poorly written paper, and reviewers do not want to read a poorly written paper'. Cornwall explains that 'catchy titles sometimes backfire'. That is because the catchier it is, the more likely accurate keywords will be missing.

An abstract's purpose is to tell browsers, searchers and indexers what a paper contains. It should attract a reader who seeks a particular kind of information or approach. Just as importantly, it should deter a reader who is seeking specific information which is not in your article. The function is, therefore, not to 'sell' your article to all and sundry, but to indicate its usefulness to the people who will benefit from reading it. It is, once again, a question of targeting your audience properly and delivering your promise.

How can you digest all your discussion into, typically, less than a hundred words? Using the following technique, distilled from professional abstractors, you can do this quickly, easily and informatively, in just three sentences.

Sentence one: the purpose

The first sentence of your abstract should restate the purpose of the paper. Abstractors say that the abstract should normally start with a verb rather than 'This paper...', which is redundant. Try verbs such as: discusses, argues, suggests, shows, studies, reviews, and so on.

For example, an abstract for this book might have as its first sentence: 'Shows how prospective authors can prepare publishable papers'.

Sentence two: the argument

This sentence summarizes the main points of your argument and the method you used. How did you show, discuss, and demonstrate? Select the main points of your argument for inclusion.

The second sentence of this book's abstract might read: 'Presents a series of frameworks which discuss selecting a prospective journal, understanding the editorial review process, structuring a paper and writing the paper, drawn largely from research studies and interviews.'

Sentence three: the findings

The third sentence summarizes what you have found. What are your main conclusions? What are some of the implications you have revealed?

The third sentence of this book's abstract might read: 'Concludes that, by following the steps and preparation described, an author can turn research and ideas into a publishable paper in a few days'.

Following this simple framework allows you to create an informative abstract for the readers of your paper, quickly and easily. And that is just one more small step towards keeping a journal's editor and publishers happy.

Post submission: accept, revise, reject

Once your paper has been submitted, a decision will be sent to you in a matter, usually, of weeks. There are usually only three options.

Acceptance

Acceptance of a paper with no revisions is a rare response. The paper will likely require minor stylistic changes, but those will be made by the copy-editing staff and will amount to little more than tidying up small sections of writing or changing headings to conform to house style. By implication, if not by direct comment in the Notes for Authors, every journal reserves this right.

Once your paper is accepted you will receive a letter telling you about the decision and an indication of which issue will carry your paper. This date may not be absolutely fixed. Too many articles in a previous issue may result in some papers being held over into the next, or in-house production schedule changes or print problems may delay the scheduled date. Some journals work to longer timescales than others, depending on the subject matter and the backlog. If it irks you to think that your paper might not appear for a year after it has been accepted, think again about the length of the review process and consider carefully whether you are prepared to risk more time and potential rejection by another journal. The editor is usually the best judge on these matters. He or she doesn't want an outdated paper in the journal any more than you do. If the editor feels the paper will still have relevance and weight in a year's time, then he or she is usually right.

Rejection

A rejected paper means that the editor and reviewers do not feel it could be appropriate for the readership even if amendments were made. While it is easy to imagine that rejection is purely a function of copy overload, the truth is somewhat different. Even if an editor has sufficient copy for the next volume, an excellent paper may still be accepted, even if the publication date is further away. The reviewers usually have no idea what the editor's backlog is, or even if there is one. They merely judge a paper on its merit.

A rejected paper tells you one of several things:

- Your paper may have been badly targeted.
- Your paper may have been badly written, badly structured, badly argued, or otherwise weak.
- Your paper may have been very good, but just not as good as some of the others.

We must assume now that, if you have done your research properly, targeted the journal correctly, structured your article, written it well and followed the journal's Notes for Authors, only the latter could possibly apply. In this case, you should find another journal with a similar readership but with a lower profile and therefore fewer competing submissions.

Revision

Assume you will be asked to revise. Few papers are accepted outright and if you have done your job properly, you should not have been rejected. It is part of the understanding when you submit a paper that you will accept referee advice.

Being asked to revise an article is a compliment and, as Prof. Linda Woodhead noted in Chapter 2, it is often the best possible advice for free. It means that you are regarded as a potential contributor to the journal and therefore also as a potential contributor to the body of knowledge. Perhaps all that is missing are a few more references, or a better explanation of your method, or a restructuring to achieve the right emphasis for the journal. Whatever the reason, the reviewers and editors feel you are worth the effort.

You should view this process as not simply extra work but as extra, free, support and advice. Everything the editors and reviewers are doing is in your best interests and the best interests of the field. At this point, everyone is working together for the benefit of other scholars and interested readers. As one reviewer commented:

> It's quite a reasonable piece in many ways, but lacks depth. It would be a pity to reject it outright and discourage the author. It just needs more work!

It would have been easier for them to have rejected your paper outright. But rather than reject you, they have decided to work with you to help you amend the article and make it better. The following quotation is one I have reread many times, simply because it shows how much a dedicated reviewer is prepared to give to a willing author:

> I have read this paper several times and, with the best will in the world, it cannot possibly be published in its current form. The argument is very badly structured, the contextual material is almost non-existent and the methodology is very poorly (albeit exhaustively!) explained. To be truthful, the manuscript is almost unintelligible as it stands. That said, there

is the kernel of a useful paper here … The author would do well to attempt to approach his/her material from the reader's perspective.

'Almost unintelligible' is not a phrase that anyone wants to hear but bear in mind that the reviewer still thinks something good might come of it all. Note that the problem in understanding has not come from the words themselves, but the lack of explicit purpose and structure. If you have worked through the previous chapters, you will be unlikely to receive a critique like the above, but even so it does give pause for thought.

How much easier it would have been for the reviewer to simply have recommended rejection; there would be little argument about the justice in that decision. Instead, the reviewer has spent time looking more deeply into the paper's potential and, by virtue of that decision, into the author's potential. For many editors, being able to help authors shape their papers is the most satisfying part of their job.

For example, Prof. Rhys Williams is an experienced editor who has edited two journals: *Social Problems* and the *Journal for the Scientific Study of Religion*. He says one of the best parts of his job is helping authors improve papers.

> For me, the most satisfying aspect of the job is seeing a paper appear in print that originally came into the journal as more potential than realized quality. The process of wrestling with the paper's ideas, interacting with the author over what revisions seem most promising, and editing the final product to help show off the paper's best features is rewarding both intellectually and interpersonally. Especially when the author is a graduate student or an assistant professor, there is also a type of paternal or avuncular pride involved.

Ask experienced authors what it is they value most in the publishing process and the answer will most often be one word: feedback. As experienced and proficient as they may be, they know they can always do better and are grateful for the insights of others who will help them improve their ability to communicate with their audience.

Unfortunately, less experienced and less wise authors can create unnecessary trouble for an editor. Once an article is marked 'revise' it will be sent back to you with an invitation to revise it within a certain period of time. What should you do then?

First, accept the comments with enthusiasm. Experienced editor Audrey Gilmore advised prospective authors that there is only way to deal with reviews: respond directly and positively. Respond to the editor immediately agreeing to make the suggested revisions by the date given. Then, without fail, stick to it. But what if you cannot? What if the comments are too fundamental to be corrected simply by rewriting parts of the paper? This is not usually the case, simply because papers which are so seriously flawed due to their original methodology or lack of evidence are usually rejected. Sometimes, the reviewer or editor suggests that such a paper can be reduced to a research note, or a report on work in progress.

Revisions are therefore changes that the reviewer thinks you can make based on his or her understanding of your work so far. But what if that judgement is wrong? What if there is nothing you can do to enhance the parts which were considered weak? Maybe the reviewer hoped you had more information which you could add to your findings, but you do not. Perhaps you glossed over the implications mainly because, upon reflection, you realized your research was so narrow and inconclusive that the findings could not be generalized or applied elsewhere.

Resist making such assumptions before talking to someone else – your supervisor, or another close colleague. Make sure you are not being overly defensive and explore deeply the critique you have received in light of all the material you have available. If, after all that, you conclude that you do not have the material available to revise the paper, then say so. Partially revising a paper which has been reviewed is worse than not revising it at all. The impression the incomplete work gives is that either you did not understand the revisions requested or you could not be bothered to make them. In either case, it does nothing to enhance your reputation as a serious researcher.

The best response now is to write back to the editor and explain the problem. Agree with the reviewer's comments but point out why and where you are unable to make the revisions. Suggest an alternative: perhaps a shorter research note, or a narrower paper focusing just on the literature, or a report on work in progress if your research is still live. The editor may reject all these ideas, but at least you have given the journal another opportunity.

Some authors at this stage choose to ignore the serious problems being noted in their manuscript and send the paper to another journal hoping that the editors and reviewers there may not notice or care. This is work that should have been done while you were targeting the journals in the first place, given that some journals will put greater or less emphasis on different quality criteria. As you had decided already that your chosen journal was the most suitable, you must ask yourself why you are not able to meet its requirements. The serious problem with sending a poor paper elsewhere is that you might be unlucky enough to get it published. Now, all your flaws and inconsistencies are not being only noticed by an editor and two reviewers but also by everyone else! Far better to reduce the paper to something else if you can, eliminating entirely the unrecoverable sections, and continue your research.

The other problem in sending the rejected or request-to-revise paper to another journal is that there is a good chance that the reviewer who was involved on the first journal, let's call it *Journal A*, will also be involved with the second, *Journal B*. Remember, reviewers are experts in their field who work independently of journals. They are based in universities or other specialist institutions and are called upon because of their expertise. Consider, for a moment, the reaction of Prof. X who has reviewed your paper for *Journal A* and put in a few hours reading it, commenting and making detailed recommendations. Now, on top of their already busy day and barely manageable workload appears a request from *Journal B* to review a paper that has recently arrived. A paper, Prof. X will immediately discern, that looks oddly familiar. Some reviewers might be more magnanimous than I, or other reviewers I know, but my guess is that Prof. X will recommend rejection.

Marie Cornwall (2010) reinforces this point by saying the biggest mistake an author can make is to ignore the review comments on a paper and simply sent it off to another journal.

As she points out, as described above, that 'the pool of reviewers is finite. The likelihood that an editor will seek out the same reviewers on the second or third submission of the same paper to different journals is relatively high. Occasionally, then, the same reviewer will review a paper for two different journals.'

A reviewer may well detect that an author has not followed review comments from a previous reading and may therefore 'give that paper less consideration on the second reading'. After all, she says, if an author has ignored the previous reviewer's comments (and, I will remind readers here, is disrespectful of that reviewer's and the journal's hard work and time) 'how does one know they can respond to a second round?' She points out that ignoring reviewer responses and just sending the paper to another journal brings with it a higher likelihood rejection.

So, let's assume you will make the wise decision and decide to revise. When you revise, do it on time. There are no excuses allowable for authors who agree to meet deadlines and then do not. Saying you are busy is an insult to busy editors and reviewers. Everyone is busy. Upon entering the review process, you made an implicit agreement to accept the judgement of the panel. They have done their job in carefully reading your work and offering you the best critique they can. Now it is your responsibility to take those comments and revise your work according to their advice and schedule.

When you are revising, take careful notes of where exactly you are making which changes because when you are finished you need to create a document summarizing your work. An editor and reviewer cannot be expected to re-read a paper line by line to try to see where you made changes and being faced with pages of 'track changes' is also daunting and difficult to understand. Create a cover note that takes each point made in the review and beside or under it write what you have done and on what page and which paragraph and line the change will be found. Yes, it is a lot of work. But a lot less than staying on the job market for years because no one will hire an unpublished academic.

Once you send your paper back to the editor it will be reviewed again. Sometimes your revisions will adequately reflect their expectations and sometimes they will ask you to go even further. The same principles as we discussed above apply to do your best to respond to their requests, tell them you are doing so, and then tell them how you have done it.

Into production

Once your manuscript has been accepted by the editorial board it will enter the production process. The manuscript must be reformatted into the journal's house style, the figures, tables and illustrations brought into the correct format and the whole paper checked for any errors which were not caught by the author or reviewers. The paper may be edited slightly for style.

The people who will make these corrections or changes are copyeditors and proofreaders. They are not subject matter experts, nor are they expected to be. As publishing has moved towards a more electronic process, some of the roles overlap.

Copyeditors

Copyeditors are valued for their language and presentation skills. They can usually be trusted to pick up awkward turns of phrase, grammatical problems, or spelling mistakes. This is a great help for authors writing in a language which is not their first. They also check for consistencies within the manuscript, ensuring that if you refer to a diagram, it is there, and it has the same title in the text as it does on the graphic; that references you cite in the text are listed at the end and in the right style; that the people to whom you refer have their names spelled correctly; and so on. They also mark up the manuscript for house style, indicating headings, subheadings, indents, and other typographical detail. Nowadays, as more publishers incorporate information technology, the copyediting process is moving from paper to screen.

This saves time and money, as fewer errors appear and reappear through rekeying.

Proofreaders

The proofreading function may be taken on by copyeditors as well, or there may be people appointed for just that job. The proofreader reads the final text for typographical errors and double-checks for consistency. If the copyeditor has done the copyediting job first, then the proofreader should not be checking for style, but rather for mistakes. Proofreading is a science, and an art. Training and extensive practice are required to develop the skills of spotting sometimes small mistakes that can be overlooked at first glance.

Author's proofs

Authors and editors are usually sent proofs of their papers. The purpose of this is to allow the author to see the final version, and check for typographical errors, but not to make extensive changes. Many publishers will charge the author for any changes made beyond typographical errors. They assume, correctly, that having been through review and possibly revision, the author and editorial board are satisfied with the paper as it stands.

The author is asked to see the proofs mainly because he or she is the best expert on the paper and may catch an error which went unnoticed by the production team. Also, the author's paper may have been edited and it is a courtesy to allow the author to see the changes. It is not, however, expected that the author will disagree with those changes unless a serious problem in understanding has arisen.

Many authors find this stage exceedingly difficult. Each time you see your work you will be tempted to change it. You will think that you could always write a little more clearly; there is always a sentence you think could be improved; there is always something more you think you can say. Of course, you are right. There is always something more. But remember the advice we heard earlier. There are perfect papers, and there are published papers. Authors must discipline themselves to let their work go. Another reason not to introduce new material is because the work will have already been through the peer review process and finally approved – what if an author were to be allowed to add new ideas post-review? As Taylor and Francis Ltd. advise their authors:

> Authors may want to add at proof stage some text on important observations made since submitting the manuscript. The decision to allow such additions must be left to the editor. Adding new content to a

peer-reviewed article under an old 'received' date is generally considered unethical if that content has not been judged for its acceptability by the peer reviewers. The editor may suggest including a dated addendum or 'note added in proof' containing the new material, which will remove the need for changes in the text.

Some publishers send authors a checklist for proofing. The main points to watch for are inconsistencies:

- Are the authors' names spelled correctly?
- Is the title of the paper correct and is it the same wherever it appears, such as on the title page and on the abstract?
- Is the institution correct?
- Are all the figures, tables, illustrations included?
- Are they correct? This is often the weak point in the production process, as it is easy to transpose figures or even the axes of graphs.
- Are figures labelled in the text as Figure 1, and so on, and does each figure have the correct label?
- Are references cited in the text listed at the end?
- Are the names of those referenced spelled correctly and consistently?
- Are footnotes correctly labelled and in the right place?

Authors are normally given only a few days to check their proofs and send them back to the publisher. Publishers will not want to delay a whole journal issue because they are awaiting proofs from one author, so as usual the deadline must be met.

A similar process exists for some funding applications which allow resubmissions and revisions.

Feedback and resubmissions for funding proposals

Sometimes, however hard you have tried, there is just not enough money to go round. The ESRC, for example, explains in its guidance notes that a rejected alpha-graded proposal means that although your proposal may be one the ESRC wanted to support 'in principle', there was just not enough money. Two-thirds of alpha-graded proposals are rejected for that reason. The ESRC also emphasizes that researchers should not assume that just because their proposal was alpha level that they should consider resubmitting 'with some window-dressing adjustments'. Resubmissions are not encouraged unless it can be shown that the proposal has been significantly revised. Before you consider taking those steps, talk to them.

If, on the other hand your proposal was rejected with a beta grade, they do not advise any resubmission. They may offer reviewer comments, but this is not given an invitation to revise and resubmit.

Funding boards usually discourage resubmissions, preferring instead to assign the proposal to another category:

A⁺   An application of the highest quality, to be funded as a matter of top priority.

A   An application of high quality, to be funded as a matter of priority.

A⁻   A good application, worthy of funding, but not as a priority.

B   Resubmit.

In some cases, funding bodies may assign the proposal to another category when they regard it as potentially fundable, but with some unresolved questions relating to a number of issues. These may include the timetable of the proposed research, the roles and responsibilities of the project team, the proposed budget, or other minor matters.

It is apparent, therefore that potential for resubmissions varies considerably from funder to funder. Some do not allow any, while others will give feedback and engage with the researchers about revising. Other funders, such as the Nuffield Foundation, may accept short, outline proposals so that the assessment can be initially swift. In practice, about 40 per cent are turned away as ineligible.

A successful funded researcher I interviewed stressed that asking for feedback is essential whether or not resubmissions are allowed. The opportunity for feedback and resubmissions will vary according to the funder and the way they organize their assessment process. They said:

> I've had as many failed bids as I've had successful bids, so I always ask for feedback about what was good and what was bad, because that helps to understand how you need to structure a bid for the future for that organisation.

The term 'partnership' will by now be familiar to readers, but its use in the sense of post-funding negotiation may be surprising. How can a funder possibly agree to fund something, which is not yet fully agreed and explored? This will, as always, depend on the funder and its approach to relationships, but it is something that a good researcher can convey throughout the proposal process. It is also one more reason to see the relationship as continuing rather than simply a one-off transaction. Just receiving a blanket yes or no does not offer room for collaboration. The researchers who conduct their funding relationships with the kind of integrity that allows the funder to invest in them first and negotiate later are, as one funder put it, those that they want to work with repeatedly.

As one successfully funded research said in reinforcing that point:

> Sometimes I've had help from the assessing panel, for example about our proposed methodology, and we've had feedback saying – wouldn't it be better to go about things in a different order, or do something slightly different, and that's been very helpful. Very often, that happens and the result is, they ask for you to resubmit your proposal along the lines that we've talked about, and we'll receive it much more favourably.

If you know the funder and have that kind of rapport, it may be possible to discuss the resubmission face to face. In one researcher's experience, the best case is to be able to have a post-proposal interview where the prospective funder and discuss the detail and offer alternatives. In one particular case for example, the funder was clear that the proposal had too many stages and could not be achieved within the budget, but if a stage was cut then the project could go ahead on the basis of a resubmission: 'When they say please resubmit, what they're saying is, you do what we discussed and we'll give it to you.'

That may sound more like ultimatum than negotiation but, as always, this varies from funder to funder. It will then be up to the researcher to decide whether, as in the above example, that stage could be cut and preserve academic integrity or whether the concept of academic integrity itself needs to be negotiated. No research proposal can be perfect due to the uncertain nature of the research process itself. Sometimes, the negotiation phase gives the proper opportunity to revisit the process.

Being open to rejection or revision means being open to change. The more you can practise talking with potential funders and renegotiating proposals, the more likely it is you will be regarded as self-confident rather than arrogant.

Summary

This chapter began by stating that an academic paper or proposal could be finished in a matter of days. It may take authors and applicants several weeks to research adequately the target journal or funder and work through the questions posed in earlier chapters. This is not, of course, weeks of doing nothing else. I assume that the author or applicant will integrate the process of finding journals and reading them into daily working life. But once you have sat down and summarized the relevant information into a synopsis you can look at the calendar and plan how you will celebrate in a week's time. Indeed, like most well-prepared authors and applicants, you will realize that the writing itself takes a fraction of the preparation time.

Any activity that appears effortless, whether it is figure-skating, opera singing, or football, only gives that impression because of the training and preparation that preceded the event. Abraham Lincoln's famous Gettysburg Address – the 'government of the people, by the people, and for the people' – lasted less than two minutes. The speaker who preceded him at Gettysburg, Edward Everett, talked for two hours. Does anyone remember him? Does anyone remember what he said?

Action points

This chapter has given numerous suggestions for ways to bring your paper to draft form. Why not review them today and start making notes? That way, you will have on file all the important questions and answers about the journal, editor, funder, reviewers, and readers. No author or applicant could ask for a more complete picture of the target journal or funder and how to get published or funded there.

References

Nature Kenya/East African Natural History Society (2022). *Journal of East African Natural*, 111. *History*. Available at: https://bioone.org/journals/journal-of-east-african-natural-history

Sharp, John, John Peters and Keith Howard (2017). *The Management of a Student Research Project*. Aldershot: Gower.

12 MANAGING RELATIONSHIPS AND ACADEMIC CAREERS

Introduction

Assuming you have followed the guidance in this book, you now have a good chance of getting your research funded and published. We could end here on a positive note about enjoying the fruits of your labours and reminding you to not waste too much time before writing your next paper or proposal. But there are other opportunities which early career academics often do not consider, possibly because they do not yet see themselves as part of the wider academic community, in relationship with others involved in the process of not only getting but facilitating publishing and funding. Given the importance of increasing the diversity of committees, boards and institutions, as explored in Chapter 5, such participation is more important than ever.

Your goal in establishing such links is the same as that running through this book: successfully getting published and funded depends on understanding your field. That is how you can successfully write the 'context' section of your paper or proposal; it is how you can evaluate quickly what is new and exciting in the current issue of a journal; it is how you will develop a tone in your writing that suggests a confidence and self-assurance that will reassure reviewers that you really do know what you are talking about, even if the current way you are talking may need some revision. Regularly publishing or getting funded requires being part of the networks of knowledge and academic activity that are necessary for any field to thrive and flourish.

The notion of 'relationship publishing' was first suggested to me as I was working on the first edition of this book by Prof. Richard Teare, then editor (and now Editor Emeritus) of *The International Journal of Contemporary Hospitality Management*. Since then, I realized it was something few new authors consider, yet many who have been involved in publishing for some time will recognize as familiar. The concept is simple: there are a limited number of journals reflecting any author's own subject area. Over time, those journals will probably become the chosen outlet for the author. Once

DOI: 10.4324/9781003259718-15

a paper has been published in a journal, the author becomes a member of a new community. If other members of that community respect the author's work, he or she may be invited to become more involved. Everyone wants to be associated with success; authors can help make that happen not only for themselves, but for others too.

By considering the relationship in its entirety we are accepting the notion of a continuing partnership – one which is not based on single transactions, but one which builds over time into a mutually rewarding experience. As Prof. Teare said:

> The author, the editor, the publisher and the reader share an interest in the value and quality of the product which they jointly create and consume. The stakeholders are dependent on each other, and the relationships are "successful" when their interests overlap.

The same concept can be applied to funding. Many authors and applicants picture themselves outside the publishing and funding process rather than being an integral part of it. Academic publishing and funding are an unusual example of a customer–supplier relationship because the suppliers – the authors and funded researchers – are the same sort of people, and quite often the very same people, who are the readers, or consumers. We tend to read the journals we write for and are able to evaluate articles against the needs we have at the time. Although this should make it easier for us to put ourselves in the place of others in the relationship, as we have seen in previous chapters it often does not in practice. It is worth taking some time to consider how you might fit into the wider publishing or funding team, and which ones you will want to belong to. This will be subjective, to some degree, reflecting your own views about what a 'good' journal or funder is and where you want to be seen. It may be worth reflecting on some of the ideas about 'excellence' and 'good' as discussed in Chapter 4.

As you know now from this book, each journal and funder look for its own particular blend and each paper or proposal fulfils those expectations in ways that conform to the journal's or funder's main objectives, that is why the nature of your relationship with different journals and funders will be different.

The question now is, do you want to keep this going, become a member of the editorial team or funding review board and contribute in a bigger way to the academic community? If the answer is yes, then we need to explore what you may need to consider in choosing your ideal team and how it will impact your career.

How to get involved in journals

There are a number of ways to become part of the journal editorial team.

Become a peer reviewer. If you have been published in a particular journal, take the time to write to the editor and thank them, their editorial team and reviewers for their help. For a successful funding application, do the same. This would usually be to the person who has taken the lead in the evaluation process, or the new contact you have to help manage your grant. You might then ask what the process is to become a reviewer for the journal or the funding body. Summarize, in a short paragraph, your research expertise by region, sub-discipline, research interests, and methodological preferences. You may not be invited to join the main editorial or funding panel in the first instance, but with successive reviews, you will increase your chances of becoming a regular member of the review community.

Review books for the journal. Many academics first contribute to an academic journal by writing a book review. You can choose to review a book either by contacting the book review editor with a suggestion or, if you are a member of a professional association, volunteering to be on their list of people to be notified about books which have arrived for review. Some people are nervous about reviewing books because they fear they have not accumulated sufficient experience or intellectual 'capital', but even if you are early in your career, you can have much to contribute. Just think about all the recent effort you put into writing a literature review. You may be more up to date with the current literature than someone more senior. You can review the sort of book you would read and recommend to your peers or students; it doesn't have to be the last controversial book from the most important person in your field.

It is easiest to follow the format for a standard book review. Begin by first summarizing its main theme and claim. It may be helpful at this stage to comment on why that theme or claim is currently important in your field, and why the author is or, in the case of an edited volume, the editor, is placed to be the ideal person (or not!) to address that theme or claim. Next, move on to summarizing contents, perhaps pausing to remark on one or two particularly interesting points or quotes or omissions. So far, readers will find it most helpful if your tone remains neutral and you are able to describe succinctly what the book is about. You then need to offer an opinion. It will be most helpful for your reader if you comment on the work that contributes to the field, or current debates, if appropriate, and where it sits amongst other similar or contradictory works in your discipline. The review usually ends by suggesting who might find it valuable – a newcomer to the field, perhaps, or maybe someone who is working at a more senior level.

Book reviews editor

Many journals appoint a book review editor responsible for commissioning and editing book reviews. Some book reviews are suggested by readers, and sometimes the Book Reviews editor reaches out to a specific academic to do a review. The number of reviews varies per journal, but the following job description issued by the *Sociological Review* gives a good overview of the responsibilities:

Responsibilities

- Soliciting at least 20 book reviews each year including selecting books and reviewers.
- Reviewing and editing book reviews from early career researchers and established scholars and seeing their drafts through to publication.
- Ensuring that book reviews meet editorial standards as well as academic standards relating to research integrity.
- Observing the *Sociological Review*'s commitment to Equality & Diversity, internationalization, and ECR support when selecting books for review and reviewers.
- Strictly observing agreed production timelines.
- Working with the Senior Communications Officer on communication and engagement activities around book reviews.
- To undertake relevant training opportunities offered by SRFL.

In their person specification, the journal notes that a broad awareness of sociology and cognate disciplines, excellent communication skills, confidence in working with people at all levels, experience with meeting deadlines and working as a team member are all essential qualities, whereas experience of editorial work is desirable, but not essential. This suggests that such a job may be a good entry-level step.

Write a research note

Some journals welcome short reports on works in progress, summaries of key findings or comments on the use of particular techniques. By 'short', editors are typically looking for papers of about 2,000 words. More detailed guidance will be given on journal websites. For example, the *Journal of Occupational and Organizational Psychology* aims to increase understanding of people and organizations at work through papers which focus both on theory and practice. Its Notes to Contributors describe Research Notes as:

Short Research Notes should be largely empirical studies. Typically, they will do one of the following:

- Replicate existing findings in a new context.
- Develop new measures and report on their reliability and validity.
- Report contradictory findings that sharpen the interpretation of existing research.
- Present new applications of an existing measure.
- Report descriptive findings or case studies that will significantly develop professional practice.
- Offer an informed and focused challenge to key elements of an existing study, theory or measure.

Research Notes are still subject to the normal review process. Indeed, some journals recommend that what has been submitted as a full paper and failed to meet the criteria of the review board may be re-worked as a Research Note.

In conclusion, the above comments about the roles of the editorial team and opportunities for publishing may help you explore the longer-term nature of a relationship in publishing.

Become your own publicist

Don't forget to do your part in helping your published paper or funded research become accessible. Many publishers offer a pre-publication service where the reviewed and corrected paper is offered on their website before being produced as part of the journal. Draw people's attention to this so they can benefit from your research weeks or months before it is 'published'. As one editorial director explained:

> Many of our journals have what we call e-first. So rather than your paper waiting in a dusty cupboard with the editor we take it and put it up online whilst it waits for a slot in the paper journal. This means it can be read earlier, cited quicker more with more hits etc. It started in the sciences, but more social science journals are going this way.

After your paper is published you can make it more widely accessible. As discussed in the opening chapter, the 'embargo' period for journals is lifted after between 12 and 24 months. That means your paper can be made more accessible through your university's Institutional Repository and through your own website. Although publishers and funders will promote your research through their website, make sure you share those pages via the most suitable platform – meta/Facebook, Twitter, Instagram, or email.

Even after your paper has been accepted and published, keep writing. Developing writing skills is like any form of training. It takes time, patience, and a regular routine to reinforce the skills. No great dancer, musician or runner performs without years of training and practice. If writing well is your aspiration, then expose yourself to people who write well. Keep yourself fit by writing regularly, even if you are not currently working on a paper. The time will come when another deadline hovers on the horizon and the last thing you want is to be out of breath after the first paragraph. People who train for physical fitness are often pleasantly surprised at how quickly the body responds and gets into shape. They are equally unpleasantly surprised by how quickly their muscles turn to flab when they stop for a few weeks. Writing is like that, too.

Most importantly, don't give up. Accept criticism and even rejection as a learning experience. As one experienced editor commented:

> It gets easier the more you do it. You pick up the rules of the game over time, and so your playing of that game becomes more skilled and much less of a struggle. Even if it's a bit of a slog at the beginning, persevere, because the more you do, the better you become. And there is a great deal of pleasure to be had in writing well about things you are interested in. There is a strong creative element which gets stronger the more experienced you become.

Join your discipline's organizations: Most disciplines, and many of the sub-disciplines, have professional organizations designed to represent the discipline to academia, universities, and sometimes government. This can be important when, for example, departments are threatened with closure. The groups also allow members to get to know each other, to meet formally and informally and to participate in events such as conferences and workshops. Many offer training in academic skills, such as getting published or funded. Some have their own publications, such as a journal or newsletter, and may also have small grants or bursaries for attending conferences. The publications offer ideal opportunities for involvement as they may be smaller and the people more accessible than some of the larger journals. It may be as simple as chatting to an editor at the group's conference to find out what is on offer and how a new member can get involved. It is also good experience in proposal writing to apply for one of the conference bursaries.

If successful, ensure to add this to the 'grants and awards' section of your CV. However small the amount, receiving it puts you in a new category of 'funded researcher'.

When attending an association's conference, check out, and attend, the 'welcome' breakfast or lunch many provide (at a small cost) for first-time attendees. This is an ideal way to network quickly with other first-timers, and often with some of the 'old-timers' who attend to give short talks. I recall one of the first 'welcome lunches' I attended at a conference that encouraged both new and established scholars. It was, I reflected later, 'like walking into my bibliography'.

All associations require volunteers to help on their committees. Several posts may be ideal for new academics: the position of postgraduate liaison, for example, or social media officer, or book review organizer are examples of posts that require help and also provide useful experience, training and profile. Remember, when applying for funding that the funder needs reassurance that you are to be trusted and, preferably, have a track record of being in responsible academic positions. Showing that you have, for example, been elected to and served for two years on a profession's committee demonstrates that you are a committed academic who is likely to fulfil obligations, such as controlling the research budget and achieving the milestones you have set for yourself. Besides, it is usually fascinating and often fun to be working closely with other academics who, like you, have found not just a career but a vocation.

Working the conference

Conferences deserve a special mention as they are occasions both to network and to promote your work.

The term 'network' needs some clarification. At one of the training events I attended when I was doing an ESRC postdoc, I'll never forget the comment made by one of the speakers: 'Networking is when you get other people to do your work for you.' That comment stayed with me, and I still think about what it means. It seems, I conclude, to relate to the theme developed extensively through this book: collaboration.

If you approach a conference as a networking and collaborating opportunity, then that means being attentive to what other people are doing. Make a point of going through the conference programme and noting those people who are engaged in similar work. You might find it helps to go further and look for those whose 'thesis' or approach and argumentation are similar to yours. Who shares your view of your field, of your future?

To collaborate effectively with someone means sharing their vision, their 'take' on the research questions that interest you both. Attending their presentation will give you further insights into their work. And then, it's simply a matter of chatting afterwards and discussing what you might do to further your mutual interests. An edited collection? A research project? A joint paper at the next conference? Organizing a panel?

And then, follow up. One of the hardest tasks after a conference is to sit down, review your notes, write emails to people you have met, and order the books you said you would read. The conference is done, you are tired from the event and possibly the travel and time difference, and the rest of your life – domestic and work – is demanding your attention.

Try to anticipate this and make a plan before you go to the conference – even something so simple as adding an appointment in your calendar as 'conference follow-up'.

One cautionary note about conferences: be aware of the consequences of giving a paper orally and of submitting it to any form of 'conference proceedings'. There are two important considerations.

First, while oral presentations can stimulate discussion, your ultimate goal needs to be larger than simply informing the handful of people who have turned up for your 'paper'. I do not recommend giving a presentation if the content is not already tied to a publication. You want your audience to be able to cite you, not just mention what you said as they chat with others in future conversations. Publication details need to be clear, preferably on your closing slide as that will stay visible for longer.

Second, remember that journals will only publish original work that has not been previously published. If you allow your paper to be included in any other published form, whether a collection of papers available on the conference website, or a bound copy of 'proceedings', it has been 'published' and therefore cannot be submitted to a journal.

Join or create a writing group

Marie Cornwall (2010), the experienced editor quoted frequently in this book, ended her 'top tips' list with advice for authors who want to improve their writing skills and quality. She explained that even good manuscripts, which have generally met the criteria for good research, will not get published if the writing is poor and the paper unstructured. She says that well-written papers are 'deceiving' because reviewers will often prefer a paper they can easily understand over one that needs work.

Her point resonates with the advice I have offered throughout this book: remember that reviewers are busy people who would rather not spend their time trying to unravel complex or grammatically incorrect, sentences.

Her recommendation on that point is unequivocal: 'Never submit a paper that has not been read by others in the field.' Sound advice, but how will that happen in practice? Everyone in your field is busy, and few have the time or inclination to read carefully and give detailed feedback on 7,000 words someone they barely know has just sent them. The solution, she explains, is to belong to 'a network of scholar friends' who are committed to reading each other's work. That, of course, requires relationships and collaborations.

Check out what is available at your university as many already have writing groups for emerging and sometimes even established scholars. It has been a practice in feminist academic circles for decades to support other women scholars by sharing and helping shape papers in practice. Many professional organizations have either writing groups or regular writing workshops and retreats. While these can be wonderful opportunities for gaining focused writing time, and I know from the many workshops I have run for decades that this inspires and rejuvenates many scholars, what is also necessary is connect with a group of scholars regularly so that people will be willing to share and advise on either other's papers. As Cornwall (2010) says: 'The most successful young scholars seek out suggestions and take recommendations seriously. Good writing requires a network of scholar friends who can tell you if the article just does not work.'

Ask them!

Many early career academics are overwhelmed and intimidated by more senior, established scholars and, by so doing, fail to recognize them as human, considerate and often very approachable. No matter how busy or overworked they feel, most academics are delighted to receive a personal note from someone commenting on their work. After all, most of us know that writing is a lonely occupation, and so to have someone mention a paper or book they have read and say what it has meant to them, comes as a welcome communication. Your purpose needs to be clear, however, your email short and your request easy to understand. Writing to one of the top people in your field and asking them if they have any ideas about books you might read is likely to get short shrift: don't you know what books to read? Why would you waste someone's time asking them? But if you intend to be at a future conference when they are, or in the city where they work within the near future, it can be worth asking them if there is an event or academic network they could recommend to help you further your career or interest.

While it is unlikely any busy academic will agree to read a paper you have just written, they may be more open to participating in an event you can organize, perhaps as a panel member or a discussant at an event.

Finally, remember what it was like before you became published or funded. There are many people in your university or on your professional networks who are still wrestling with their concerns and fears. Perhaps volunteer to organize a writing group where people can review each other's papers before sending them to a journal. At the very least, be available. This book would never have been written were it not for the kind assistance and expert advice given by editors, reviewers, publishers, funders, authors, funded researchers. Join them!

Summary

The book's concluding chapter has tried to summarize many of the themes that have run throughout this book by connecting them to an academic's long career. Although many of the above points may appear useful, they are only a partial list and will undoubtedly change over time as the publishing industry changes and as the funding landscape adapts to new challenges and ways of working.

What will not change, I suspect, is the constant need to stay connected, to stay a part of an academic community and to collaborate in ways that help the community, and your career, grow.

Action points

1. Review your favourite journal's website to assess where there may be opportunity for your involvement – peer reviewer? Book reviewer? Section editor?

2. Contact the journal editorial team to see how to involve yourself in their different activities.

3. Review the website of funder's and see where they offer opportunities for further involvement, perhaps in contributing to a blog or research note. Most funders give detailed guidance about how to publicize your research. Contact them directly if you feel you need help further promoting your funded research, or to assist in an event or other dissemination activity. Be proactive and persistent.

INDEX